THE SUNDAY TIMES

Don't Panic!

THE SUNDAY TIMES

Don't Panic!

Answers to All Your Computer Problems

Nigel Powell

with cartoons by
Nick Newman

TIMES BOOKS

Published in 2004 by Times Books

HarperCollins*Publishers*
77-85 Fulham Palace Road
Hammersmith
London W6 8JB
www.collins.co.uk

Printing 10 9 8 7 6 5 4 3 2 1 0

The Sunday Times is a registered trademark of
Times Newspapers Ltd

ISBN 0-00-719027-1

British Library Cataloguing in Publication Data
A catalogue record for this book is available from the
British Library

Typeset in Great Britain by
Davidson Pre-Press Graphics Ltd, Glasgow

Printed and bound in Great Britain by
Clays Ltd, St Ives plc

Contents

A Word of Thanks

A huge thank you to the Doors team at *The Sunday Times* and especially my editor David Johnson, father of the 'Don't Panic' column and enthusiastic driving force behind the creation of this book. Thanks also to Meta and Emily for their support, Adam and Georgia for cheerleading and Nick and the Toshiba team for help when it really counted. A big doff o' the cap also to Christopher Riches at HarperCollins who has patiently and professionally steered this book through to completion. But of course the biggest thanks must go to all the wonderful Don't Panic readers, without whom none of this would have been possible.

Dedicated to my Mother.

Top 20 Don't Panic questions

- Is it possible to retrieve email messages that have been deleted from the Deleted Items folder in Outlook Express? (*see page 50*)
- My internet browser's start page has been hijacked to display another site. When I change it back, it returns after an hour or so. What can I do? (*see page 84*)
- I have 30 CD-R disks full of photos but some have been corrupted even though they are stored away from light and heat. Any advice? (*see page 216*)
- What is the best way to maximise the life of a laptop computer's battery? (*see page 185*)
- What are the best options for upgrading my VHS recorder? (*see page 326*)
- What is the most efficient way to back up my computer? (*see page 188*)
- What is the best way to transfer music from cassette onto CD? (*see page 226*)
- I cannot make the defragmentation program work on my Windows 98 computer. Is there any alternative? (*see page 160*)
- Is there a charity that will accept old PCs and printers for use in schools here or in poorer countries? (*see page 183*)

- I recently bought an American DVD that will not work in my player because it is for the wrong region. What can I do? (*see page 327*)
- My new PC keeps freezing. What can I do? (*see page 184*)
- What are zip files and how do you use them? (*see page 261*)
- I can't get the sound to work on my PC, despite trying everything I can think of to fix the problem. What am I doing wrong? (*see page 176*)
- Is there any way to stop the horrible screeching noise when my modem connects to the internet? (*see page 149*)
- How do I convert my MP3 files so I can save them to a music CD and play them through my home system? (*see page 281*)
- Is there a simple way to transfer my entire email Outlook Express book and messages from one computer to another? (*see page 56*)
- What is the cheapest way to access the internet when I'm abroad? (*see page 84*)
- Why can't I open attachments in my AOL mail? (*see page 49*)
- Why does my PC keep disconnecting from the internet for no apparent reason? (*see page 86*)
- All the digital photos I send via email are enormous when opened. How can I get round this? (*see page 52*)

Introduction

Technology is fun. OK, a few irritating things can happen, such as computers that shudder and crash, and video recorders that insist on taping the wrong programmes no matter how carefully we set them. But, in general, the rise and rise of electronic aids has benefited us all. Who could have imagined just ten years ago that we could set up a video link between families thousands of miles apart, using nothing more sophisticated than a phone line, a basic PC and a £30 webcam?

Unfortunately the growth in technology for the home has also created a mishmash of rules, standards, instruction manuals and compatibility, which can make the process of buying and using this wondrous new equipment a nightmare of Dantean proportions. Which is where I hope this book will be of use. Take comfort in its pages, as you wearily sift through yet another tangled mess of cables and manuals, cocoa in hand and expletive on lip.

Dip into the relevant section when you stumble across a question for which there seems no rational answer. I cannot guarantee a complete solution at every turn, but hopefully most sections will furnish answers to the type of general queries you will come across from time to time. I have also tried to include as many links to information sources as possible to cover those situations where an answer is not immediately apparent.

Regular readers of my *Sunday Times* Don't Panic column will know that the main aim is to present technological solutions in a jargon-free way and so avoid adding more confusion to the pot. The column and now this book were created from a desire to assist technology users from every walk of life and every age group – our youngest correspondent to date has been 11 years old, the oldest over 90. Each question has been chosen on the basis of two main criteria: is it likely to trouble a sizeable proportion of the population, and is it something that can be solved by someone relatively inexperienced?

This means that you will not find answers to arcane questions of computer programming or hardcore tech issues. Nor will you come across many questions which relate to a particular model of equipment. The Don't Panic mission is a truly democratic one – technology for all.

So how do I recommend that you use this book? First and foremost, it is intended to be an easily navigated reference source for major problems affecting day-to-day users of computers and technology. It is divided into the topics which have most troubled our readers, such as email, Windows and emerging technologies such as the internet. Each section contains a short introduction, some tips and a selection of the most popular answers culled from the Don't Panic columns over the years.

The index is a good place to start your search – questions

relating to, say, Outlook Express have been grouped under the same heading as much as possible. One day someone will come up with a search engine for books; until then we will have to live with the imperfections of thumbing pages and running our eyes down lines of print. Having located the subject you seek, you can browse the answer section and delve into the mysterious knowledge that lies within.

One request. Please do not fling the book angrily at the wall if the solution to your problem has been omitted through the oversight of this poor scribe. The web links I give may hold the solution even if it is not specifically addressed in the book, so take the time to visit one of these if you can. Of course, if you still get no joy, you can always write to me at *The Sunday Times*. I can't promise to answer all questions sent in, but if there is enough demand for a particular issue, I do try to cover it sooner or later.

One of the questions I'm often asked by the people who pin me against walls at cocktail parties (not that I attend many, you understand; I'm much too busy rewiring hard drives etc) is whether we make up the questions used in the paper. The answer is an unequivocal no. We may sometimes gather a selection together to build a week's theme, and I generally have to reword them to squeeze long requests into tight spaces, but by and large what you read is what is asked.

The answers used in the book have also been edited in a few instances. For one thing, I've had to tidy up overlaps in topics, which are bound to occur when you're collating questions over a four-year period. In addition, although we try to unearth fresh questions ever week, there are times when it's necessary to revisit important topics, either because the technology has changed, the problem has become more acute or the old advice is outdated. Questions about anti-virus programs are a good example. For the book, I've tried to avoid repetition, but where there are two answers on a similar subject which provide different solutions I felt it was in the public interest to retain both.

A final note on computer problems. In all of this, it pays to remember one thing – technology exists as a tool for us to use, not the other way round. Once we understand that even the most complex computer system is basically nothing more than a rather large calculator, we can start to overcome our reluctance to experiment and enjoy the potential of these marvellous beasts. Contrary to common belief, computers very rarely explode in a shower of sparks and flame. In my experience, the sound you come to fear most is a soft sigh and an all but inaudible splut. At which point I usually reach for the spare-parts catalogue.

If I had to offer a single piece of guidance on tackling computer issues, it would be to take things one step at a time. In many instances, the cause of a problem can be traced directly to the addition of new software or hardware. Did the problem occur after you installed that new printer or photo-

editing software? Then that is probably causing the problem.
Try uninstalling it, or visit the manufacturer's website and
see if others have reported a problem with your type of
configuration. Often all that's needed is the installation of
a new driver (see computer hardware).

And, above all, Don't Panic!

1 · Choosing and buying a computer

A few years ago I was travelling home from a meeting in central London on the Underground and noticed a middle-aged couple opposite me avidly reading some product literature. When I looked closer I saw that it was from a computer company in West London. Ever the nosy type, I leaned over and started a conversation with them, introducing myself as 'someone who writes about computers'. Having recovered from the shock of being accosted by an ugly brute in a naff blue jumper, they very politely confirmed they were indeed off to buy a computer.

'Have you been looking long?' I asked.

'Well,' said the lady, 'we've bought a book, we've been to some shops, and now we're going to a factory to see what they have to offer.'

At that moment, as I thought back to my own first attempt to buy a computer, it struck me that most of us go through the same sort of process.

First we decide we need one. We have a specific idea in mind, whether it is to write a book, start a small home-based business, learn about graphic design or help the children with their education.

We check the bank statement to see how much we can

spend, then buy two or three computer magazines from the newsagent, the thicker the better. We read them, or rather skim through pages of adverts, trying to pick out product reviews and definitions which will help us grasp what we need to know.

We may chat to a friend we know to be 'in the business' or colleague at work who is an enthusiast. More often than not, the result of these conversations is a guarded recommendation to 'take a look at such and such, they're not bad…' (Anyone who knows about computers is well aware of the dangers of wholeheartedly recommending a particular product.)

Finally, we start trudging and ringing round to whittle down the alternatives and make our choice. By this stage, we may know a bit more about what the task entails than we did in the beginning, or we may be just as confused as when we started.

If you're like me when I bought my first computer more than 24 years ago, your head will be swimming with terms such as RAM, ROM, megahertz, gigabytes, memory, disk storage and the like. Some of it will make a kind of sense, other parts will still be complete gobbledygook.

This section is my attempt to make a little sense of the nonsense you may find out there in computer land. At the very least, it should give you a grounding in the basics of computing and enough knowledge to avoid being sneered at by some smarmy salesman in a showroom.

Try to remember one thing though: despite what industry pundits would have you believe, the computer is nothing more than a big calculator. Fast, flexible and expensive maybe, but a calculator nonetheless. Don't be intimidated by the technology and you may find it opens up unexpected new areas of creativity in your life.

The checklist

Nobody expects you to be a computer programmer in order to buy a PC, any more than you have to be a mechanic to buy a car. However, there are some basic things it is important to know. You wouldn't buy a car without asking about miles per gallon, performance speed and general handling, would you? Computers also have some fundamental features, which basically relate to speed and space: speed of processor, speed of CD ROM, speed of graphics, size of memory, size of hard disk storage, size of monitor and so on.

But before you buy there are probably only three key areas to keep in mind.

What are the hardware options, and what do they mean?

The hardware consists of the actual 'hard' pieces which make up the system. This includes the keyboard, which is used to

input data; the monitor, which is the equivalent of
a television screen, and the computer system unit, which
is usually a square box in which the computer's 'engine'
resides.

Processor

The processor (or CPU, which means central processing unit)
is the brain of the computer and does most of the key
calculation work. Processor speeds (1GHz, 2.8GHz etc) are
the equivalent of the size of the car engine. We need to know
whether our car is capable of cruising effortlessly to work
every morning or if it will chug along and struggle up the
slightest incline. The processor speed provides the equivalent
information – the bigger the number the faster it should be.
Note, however, that processor manufacturers such as Intel are
talking about using brand names as a CPU identifier instead
of speed markings. Instead of buying a Pentium 4.3GHz
chip, we will be expected to buy a Pentium 7 'Rustler' or
something. We'll see how it works in practice, but for now
speed is still the common denominator.

A quick word on benchmarks

These are a set of standard tests industries adopt as a guide to comparative performance of competing products. They are used to compare processors, video cards and a host of add-on products such as printers. Despite their usefulness in comparing rough levels of performance between rival equipment, my advice is to beware of buying a computer based solely on benchmark results.

That's because bald figures often do not give a complete view of the machine's capabilities. Just because a PC can finish a task in a certain amount of time, does not mean it will be adequate for your particular task. Speed is just one of many factors which are important in judging the way a computer operates. In the same way that you would rarely buy a car just because it goes faster than another, it is unwise to purchase a PC based on processor performance alone.

Some PCs are fast but use cheaper or lower specification components, which may create problems down the line. A good example is the use of low-grade memory chips in PC RAM. The computer may look as though it has the right

kind of speed specification, but this cheaper, slower RAM
may well mean it doesn't perform as well as expected or that
it suffers reliability problems later.

Memory

RAM (random access memory) is measured in megabytes
(MB) or gigabytes (GB) and you can think of it as the
'kitchen table' where the PC does all its work. Every time
you start up a software program on your machine, the system
accesses the hard disk (see below), finds the program and
transfers the core part of it into RAM, which makes for faster
and easier access. In simple terms the memory space is used
for temporary storage of the program while it is running, so
the more memory you have in your machine, the faster and
more efficiently your programs should run.

If your kitchen table is too small, you will be able to
prepare only a small amount of food at a time and will have
to keep moving it to other parts of the kitchen to free up table
space and trudge back and forth to the cupboard to bring
more ingredients to the table for preparation. If you think of
software programs as computer food you should begin to
understand the analogy.

The amount of memory in the computer (eg 512MB
RAM) tells us how efficiently it will run our programs.
Again, the bigger the number the better. Without enough
RAM, the computer may run a lot slower than we want or

may not be able to run some large software packages at all, so always buy as much as you can afford.

Hard disk storage

This is the filing cabinet where the PC stores programs and data so you can use them when needed. It is where software programs are kept when you install them and it is currently measured in gigabytes. The amount of storage (eg a 40GB hard disk) tells us how much information our computer's internal filing cabinet can hold. Every time we save a game or a letter we've written on the computer, we use up a portion of our hard disk space. Over time this mounts up, but storage typically only really becomes a problem when we start filling up the computer with long-term work.

How to tell RAM and hard disk memory apart
One of the most confusing aspects of a PC tends to be understanding the difference between memory (RAM) and hard disk storage. When I first started using computers, I was constantly jumbling up the two in my mind when talking about specifications. A good rule of thumb is that RAM memory is only a temporary operating area and, therefore, normally a fraction of the size of a hard

disk, which is used for permanent storage of data and programs. So when faced with two capacity figures which look similar (eg 512MB and 500GB), the smaller (512MB) will invariably relate to RAM, while the larger probably indicates a hard disk.

Graphics

The video system is often a small plug-in board or card inside the machine, which transfers information from inside the computer to the screen via a cable. The better the graphics system, the faster and clearer the picture you get on the monitor. A fast, powerful video card can give the whole PC a snappier, snazzier feel. These are measured in bits – 32bit, 64bit, 128bit and so on. Note also that video cards have their own stash of memory or RAM, so remember to look for as much as possible (nowadays 128MB is becoming standard, although some cheap systems will have just 64MB).

The video is only really important for those of you who are going to be using the PC for multimedia, video editing or top-notch games. In these cases you will need the fastest and best configured graphics capability you can afford so the CD ROM, DVD or game operates smoothly and quickly.

Many modern PCs have the video card embedded in the system, not on a separate board. The basics remain the same, however, and you should always ask whether the graphics function can be upgraded if necessary by adding an extra board (usually via what's known as an AGP slot).

Those are the key features of a computer that we should know about before we begin. The remaining options, such as keyboards, DVD recording drives and the like are less important and can be thought of as options like metallic paint on a car.

A brief note on ink-jet printers

The key features of these little marvels are speed and cost of printing. The cheaper the printer, the slower it will be, especially when printing colour pages or photographs. Try to work out how much you will be using the printer and what you will be doing with it. If you are just going to print the occasional letter or text page, a cheaper model may be fine. However if you intend to print lots of digital photographs, you should seriously consider something more expensive. Check the cost of the ink cartridges too, as you may be surprised just how expensive it can be to run the cheaper models.

Notice that I have not mentioned resolution. This is because most ink-jet printers will produce excellent quality results for most purposes, which means it is only really worth paying for a top model if you need a special feature such as A3-sized output, double-side printing or a super high speed, in which case you might also consider colour laser printers.

Now we come to the central issue relating to your proposed purchase.

What do I want to do with my computer?

This is the single most important question you can ask when planning to buy a computer, because it will determine exactly what you will need. Let's make a few things clear.

If you only want to do simple things, you will only need a simple computer. This may sound obvious, but it is something that cannot be repeated often enough, especially in front of a cocky PC salesman. If you are just going to use it to write letters or reports or for any general word processing, you can get away with a relatively low specification system. By that I mean you will be able to save money by buying a PC with less RAM, a smaller hard disk, a simple video graphics card and a lower speed processor.

Remember, though, that if you intend to do anything more exciting later on – such as run the latest games or manipulate large databases of information – you may find yourself wishing you had bought something a little more powerful. It pays to think ahead when you're investing in a personal computer.

The more exotic the things you want to do on your computer, the more you will have to spend, or you will lose out on output quality and speed. If you want to compose complex music, create professional quality digital photographs or even provide your child with an interesting audio and visual platform for learning about computers, you will need to do more than just add a couple of speakers and a DVD drive. And this means spending more on the whole system.

To handle modern multimedia such as large sound, video or animation files, you will need a computer that will cope with developments which may be right around the corner. This means getting the fastest CD ROM or DVD drive, the fastest processor and the largest hard disk you can afford. You will also need a top-line video graphics system to cope with the sophisticated colour imaging on screen.

The options

There are really only three major computer configurations to choose from, and they are generally identified more by price than specification.

Entry level PC This is a PC which is at the bottom of the price scale. It will contain less RAM than the others, a smaller hard disk and slower graphics system. It may also come with a conventional CRT 'tube' type monitor. It probably will not include sophisticated features such as a DVD-RW burner (or recorder).

Mid-range PC This is traditionally the most popular because it is more future proof, with a faster processor, more storage and more default niceties such as DVD-RW, WiFi or Bluetooth wireless networking and a larger – probably flat-screen LCD – monitor. You will spend perhaps 50 per cent to 70 per cent more on this system.

Top-end PC This is the machine for those where money is probably no object, offering high specification and performance with one or more state-of-the-art features. The Ferrari of the computing world with a price to match, it typically costs around four times as much as the budget models.

No matter how technology develops, these price/specification points seem to remain constant. All that happens is you get a better specification for the money. As technology moves on, you will find low-end PCs contain the features and specifications found only in high-end PCs not so long ago. And so on.

Why you should ask for a demonstration

Do ask to see the kind of thing you will use the PC for. If you want to do word processing, take a look at – even try out – a relevant system. Is the software simple to understand? Most will have a lot of complex features, but is it, say, easy to start writing a letter immediately?

If you will be making use of a lot of multimedia software, check out a system running some. Does the screen suffer from 'jerko-vision', seeming to judder every few seconds as the program or video is playing? This could be caused by a slow CD or DVD drive, too little RAM or a processor that's too slow. Find out by trying the same software on another machine with a higher specification.

Don't be afraid to ask to see different software run on the machine. If you're evaluating the PC as a multimedia machine, take along a popular CD ROM or DVD such as Microsoft's Encarta or a film to get an idea of how it compares on different systems.

Does this fit in with my budget?

Of course this question is fairly obvious but it bears repeating here, mostly because there are a few things you can do to balance your budget against expectations.

Money v performance

How much is a little extra speed worth to you? Unless you're going to be working full time on the PC, running your business and saving the world, it is highly unlikely the slightly slower speed of an 2.8GHz processor versus a 3.4GHz is going to make much difference to your life. And by buying just below the latest state-of-the-art performance level you can usually save a significant amount of money.

Money v specification

How much is a better specification worth to you? Is that 21-inch monitor really necessary to your well-being? Can you do without an extra firewire or USB port? In general, I would suggest you sacrifice the gaudier options and instead add more memory, a larger hard disk and/or a snappy graphics card, in that order.

Money v name

This is one of the thorniest questions facing today's PC purchaser. Should I buy a well-known brand or a 'no-name' machine which is cheaper and therefore gives me more for my money? Try to decide on the product by looking at the whole company rather than just the brand name. There are a number of British manufacturers who have good user reputations even though they are not household brands, and there are a number of Far Eastern and American no-name companies who also have established a reputation over the years for providing reliable equipment. Magazine awards, size of company turnover and the like will help point the way, as will some of the more helpful PC magazines or national newspapers.

Doing an internet search on a brand of computer you are thinking of buying can often save a lot of heartache – not to mention backache – especially if you discover a large number of dissatisfied users sounding off in chat forums across the globe.

Some thoughts on support

On-site warranty agreements, where a maintenance engineer comes to your home to fix the fault, make sense. Do not buy a computer without buying some sort of on-site guarantee, especially if you are a first-time user. You may never need the service, but that maintenance guarantee levels the playing field between brand names and no-names or between the cheaper models and the Rolls-Royce alternatives. A telephone support service for your software programs can also be very helpful if you have a problem, but be prepared to pay a fairly stiff rate for phone calls. Some companies offer better deals than others, so check around.

Summary

As a guide to which computer to buy, I would suggest the following:

Simple tasks

An entry level PC for the totally budget constrained, a mid-range one for a speedier, more future-proofed system. This should be suitable for word processing or any other simple text manipulation such as producing a basic newsletter or booklet; home accounts or basic spreadsheet book-keeping; information management, such as a computerised Filofax or calendar system; basic internet access and email.

Complex tasks

A mid-range PC for office type functions, but a high-end

model is really mandatory for games, heavy multimedia use and video editing. These are the choices if you want to carry out large-scale multimedia tasks such as watching DVDs or CD ROMs; complex brochure production or design and illustration with lots of photos, graphics and artwork; sophisticated accounting with stock control and similar features; intensive internet activity such as downloading large files and documents or accessing or developing complex multimedia sites; video editing, semi-professional digital photography or other large file manipulation; state-of-the-art video gaming.

The truth about obsolescence

First things first. What do we mean by obsolete? A senior executive at one of the world's largest technology companies once joked with me that a PC is obsolete almost as soon as it comes to the end of the factory conveyer belt. While that's clearly a bit of an exaggeration, there's no doubt computers age faster than the latest teenage fashion craze. The important thing to remember is that obsolescence does not mean your computer stops working in six months. It only comes into play if you want to change how you use it and the new use requires a higher specification. In other words, buy wisely and it shouldn't be an issue for a good few years. If you are happy with the computer you bought and it still does what you want it to do, is its age really a problem?

Portable computers

No discussion of buying computers would be complete without mentioning laptop or notebook versions. In recent years the power of these svelte wonders has increased to the extent that there is very little difference in many cases between the capability of a portable and a desktop model. For this reason, most of the same principles we have looked at apply to portables. Processors, memory and storage size and quality of build all matter.

However, if you are planning to use your laptop as a true portable – you might be surprised to learn just how many people, me included, use their laptop only as a static desktop PC replacement – things like weight and battery life clearly become very important. The keyboard should not be too much of a compromise, the screen should be clear enough to read in an averagely lit room and the integrated pointing device should be easy to use. Do beware of flimsy designs.

A notebook is likely to take a lot more punishment than a desktop, so you need to invest in one that will not suffer cracked screen hinges or loose keys after a few months.

Apple Macintosh

US company Apple manufactures one of the most elegant and popular computer ranges in the world. Users rave about its beautiful design and millions have been sold around the world, mostly to creative people who don't want to be burdened in their work by what they consider primitive PCs.

Nowadays, however, the primitive PC has largely caught up with the Apple in terms of ease of use, and the latest versions of Windows XP look every bit as swish as the Apple alternative. The PC may still be the ugly duckling at the designer ball – especially when compared to something like the stunning iMac – but it remains significantly cheaper than equivalent Apple machines and, more important, has a huge amount of software available for it, including all major Macintosh design software such as QuarkXPress and Adobe Photoshop.

I tend to recommend Apple computers to home users only if they have a particular fondness for them and/or have used them enjoyably in the past. While they are still the most popular type of computer in industries such as design and music, for home use they remain hampered by a relatively high price, limited add-ons and smaller software base.

However, quite a few specialist shops supply Apple systems and software, and there is no question Apple is a hugely popular and very important part of the computing scene around the world, so do take a look at the comparative models when you're on your quest for a new computer. You may find you prefer their look and feel to the boring beige or black of other manufacturers, and who could blame you?

How to buy

High street

One of the most popular methods of buying a PC is through your nearest high street retailer. This means either a small independent trader or one of the big chains such as PC World. Smaller outlets can often devote a lot of time and expertise to your problem or needs. But you can never be sure how long the independent will remain in business, especially in a tough economic climate.

Buying from a big chain can give you the security of knowing it will be around for a while, but the staff are likely to be over stretched and you will be one of thousands vying for their time. Anyone who has waited hopelessly for attention in an electronics superstore will know exactly what I mean. Ask neighbours, friends and work colleagues if there are any companies which have a good reputation for supporting their customers in your area.

Direct sales

The mail-order computer market is huge nowadays, made especially popular by the success of Dell Computers. Open any computer magazine and you will see a huge number of small mom-and-pop manufacturers selling their wares off the page.

A rule of thumb here is that if your computer works well, you can save thousands of pounds by buying in this way. However if it goes wrong, this can quickly become a fool's saving, as you wend your way wearily through a succession of 'please hold' telephone voice systems, trying to get the problem sorted out. I'm not saying every company is like that, but it is undeniable that the cheaper the mail-order product, the more probable it is the technical support has had to be cut to the bone to ensure the company makes a profit. Even where it offers a reasonable telephone technical support service, you will probably find yourself paying upwards of £1 a minute for the privilege.

Internet

To make things even more complicated, in recent years many of the 'big brand' computer companies have started direct sales operations, mostly using the internet, to compete with the likes of Dell. Companies such as Toshiba, Fujitsu-Siemens and Hewlett Packard now sell their full range online in association with their network of regional dealers, and this can make for some good savings if you shop around.

The advantage of using these company sites is you can choose your system at leisure and make the most of any special offers, staying safe in the knowledge that you're buying from a reputable company. The disadvantage is you have no opportunity to try out the machine and must rely on a written description to satisfy your questions.

It can pay to do a quick internet search for online reviews before you buy, especially those from actual users rather than professional reviewers. Sites including *www.epinions.com* and *www.itreviews.co.uk* often contain useful write ups on particular models, which can help enormously when you're trying to make up your mind. Just do a search on *www.google.com* for the model you're interested in plus the word review. 'Toshiba Tecra 9000 review', for example, will turn up a series of opinions of this model which may help you make a decision.

Conclusion

Whatever your reason for buying a computer, hopefully you are now clearer about what to look out for and how to avoid being fobbed off with something that doesn't suit your needs. The big thing to remember is that computers are no more complex than your washing machine, they've just got more bits and pieces in them (and don't handle detergent as well), so don't let the techno talk put you off.

As long as you have a fairly good idea of how you will be using the PC and are confident your needs will not change much in, say, a couple of years, you should be able to make a sensible choice of model.

Good hunting, and have fun!

2 · Managing email

How did we ever live without email? Actually quite well as I remember, although licking all those stamps did leave an unpleasantly furry taste in the mouth. That has now been replaced by the trials and tribulations of communication at the speed of light: email-borne viruses, junk messages by the digital bucket load and, above all, that nagging urge to answer every message as quickly as possible lest we be considered rude.

There's no doubt, though, that email is a boon. When we look back, we will cherish the memory of the first time we were able to send instant digital photographs of our newborn to every relative on the far flung family tree, and wonder how we ever managed our communications using only the telephone or quill pen. In future, of course, we'll have to put up with all sorts of new fangled technology such as video messages, which may make us wish that we hadn't thrown away that bottle of Quink, but for now, email remains the champion of the new technology age.

Keen-eyed readers will note just how wide ranging the questions in this section are, a reflection perhaps of the fact that we routinely use email for a host of purposes far beyond the original intention of its creators. Transferring files, sending photos, marketing products, delivering maps and tickets are just some of the new uses of this modern telegraph system.

Top Don't Panic email tips

Protect your privacy

Be cautious about the use of your email address online.
Handing it out indiscriminately on websites or in public chat
rooms is like begging junk email merchants to plague you.
Unless you enjoy receiving unwanted advertising for all sorts
of products you will never use, it is better to be safe than sorry.

Get another address

If you do a lot of web surfing, consider signing up for a free
web email address from a provider such as Yahoo! or Hotmail.
You can give this out secure in the knowledge that you can
filter out the junk messages or ignore that particular inbox for
months at a time. If you already have a Hotmail or other web
account, consider setting up an additional public address.

Check your inbox

If you are new to email, remember to check your inbox
regularly. There's nothing more useless than sending out a raft
of 'Hey I'm now online, mail me' messages to your friends
and relations then forgetting to check your inbox for replies.

Make the most of it

Learn how you can use email to send more than just text

messages. You can use the attachment feature of most packages to send anything from digitised photos to music clips of little Emily singing *The Sound of Music*. Email is a wonderful invention and can unite remote friends and family in a way that few other things – including the telephone – can.

Improve your typing

If you plan to use email regularly, do learn to type. There are any number of good software programs which can help, probably the best of which is Mavis Beacon Teaches Typing (*www.mavisbeacon.com*). Invest a few minutes a day in learning and you won't regret it.

Top Don't Panic email questions

Q Is there any way to hide the addresses when I want to copy a message to a group of my friends in Outlook Express?

A One way is to address the message to yourself first in the To: box then click on the cc icon to access the 'blind carbon copy' (bcc) function of Outlook Express. Insert your group addresses in the bcc box and the recipients will only see your name in the To: box. You may have to explain why you enjoy writing to yourself, but hopefully that will be a minor inconvenience. I usually use this trick when I send out letters begging for cash.

Q I seem to have been added to some junk email list and am now being deluged with around 20 junk mails a day.

A Download the Spam Inspector program from *www.spaminspector.com*. There's a free 30-day trial version available, after which you will need to register for around £12. It is very powerful, though, so be cautious at first to make sure it is not filtering out mail messages that it shouldn't.

Q Please could you explain how I can transfer files from floppy disk to email to send to people?

A To send a file to someone using an email message, you need to 'attach' it to the message. The process varies according to the computer and email package you are using, but the principle remains the same.

Using Outlook Express under Windows, for instance, create the mail message you want to send then, while still editing, click Insert – File Attachment. A box pops open allowing you to browse your hard disk (or floppy disk). Having selected the file, it is automatically formatted for transmission and is sent the next time you log on to send and receive mail.

Be careful though, because files of 1.5MB and above can clog up the recipient's line and in extreme cases cause their machine to crash. It is polite to ask first before sending large files and photos.

Q How can I minimise the amount of spam email I receive?

A The most effective way to ensure you don't receive spam – also known as junk email – is to refuse to give out your email address. I'm sure you will spot the problems inherent in this action, as I did eventually after a number of years of eerily empty in boxes.

A more practical alternative is to be extremely careful about using your address in public places, such as when posting a message in a newsgroup or chat room. One good wheeze is to sign up for an additional free mail account from someone like Hotmail (*www.hotmail.com*) for logging onto websites and other public areas.

If you already suffer from a lot of unwanted email, there is little you can do. Never reply to a spam mail asking to be taken off their list, as this will simply confirm your address is a 'live' one, encouraging the sender to sell it on to others, making the situation much worse.

Q **Every week I receive at least one email message offering diplomas and qualifications. Are these legitimate?**

A File these messages in the 'too scam-tastic to be true' folder. They are worthless offers, providing useless qualifications from dubious or non-existent colleges. Far better to check out proper places like The Open University at *www.open.ac.uk/*. Here you can study at your leisure and know that you will receive a proper degree which is recognised by more than just your local chip shop.

Q **Is there a way to have a more visible notification of newly arrived emails when using Outlook Express?**

Take a look at the PopTray program (*www.poptray.org/*). This tiny free utility will monitor your email accounts and notify you when messages arrive at your ISP's mail server. It also comes with a choice of voices that announce 'You have mail' in a cheesy mid-Atlantic drawl.

Q **I use Outlook Express and would like to set up an email address for my wife. Could you please enlighten me?**

A True email enlightenment comes only with years of patience and dedication, I'm afraid. In the meantime, try clicking File – Identities – Add New Identity. From here you can follow the instructions to set up a new email account on the machine and even allocate a password to it. Do note that the password protection is not foolproof – to ensure other users will not be able to access your messages you must log out of your identity every time you quit Outlook Express. A more detailed explanation can be found at *http://support.microsoft.com/default.aspx?scid=kb; enus;209169.*

Q **How can I stop the >>> marks in my email messages?**

A These 'original message' quote marks are offered as an option in most mail programs. To turn them off in Outlook Express go to Tools – Options – Send and switch them off via the Plain Text Settings box. To strip them from text when they arrive in any email inbox, use Tahir Belenli's StripMail from *www.dsoft.com.tr/stripmail/*. It's free and simple to use.

Mac users can download EmailCleaner at *www.elfdata.com/emailcleaner/*.

Q **I plan to change my ISP and hence my email address. How can I send a private message to all my friends announcing the change?**

A If there are not too many names you could simply send the notification mail to yourself and bcc (blind carbon copy) it to all your friends. Just enter their addresses into the bcc box with a semi-colon after each one, then they will not see the others on the list. If you are wildly popular, you may need to use the free MailReactor list manager software from *www.daansystems.com*.

On a similar subject, check out the excellent free online service *www.ihavemoved.com*, which lets you notify friends, public utilities and various companies of your change of address when you move. Fill in your old address, the new one and select the people you want to notify and it is all done automatically when you're ready. Most of the major services have signed up, including the Passport Office, DVLA, gas and electricity companies and the Inland Revenue.

Q I have accidentally blocked a relative's emails and it is very annoying. Is there any way of undoing this?

A In the later versions of Outlook Express you can unblock senders simply by accessing the Tools – Message Rules menu option and clicking on Blocked Senders List. You will see a list of those you have blocked and can remove them as desired. This is a terribly useful function for the emotionally volatile who go through several kiss and make up sessions a month.

Q Why can't I open attachments in my AOL mail?

A The problem lies with the way some of the older AOL software handles email and attachments. Suffice to say there were problems with file attachments over a certain size if the sender was from outside the AOL community or sending from an AOL connection within an office environment. There is no way round this except to upgrade your AOL software – which in itself can be a hazardous exercise – or to use a file compressor such as Winzip for the PC (*www.winzip.com*) or Stuffit (*www.stuffit.com*) on the Apple Mac to make the attachment smaller. Note both parties will need this to compress and uncompress the files.

Q **How can I retrieve my Hotmail messages using Outlook Express?**

A The people at Microsoft have included a neat menu option inside the latest version of Outlook Express which allows you to set up a new Hotmail account from scratch. Select Tools – New Account Sign up and follow the instructions in the set up wizard. Once you have set things up using this service all your Hotmail email will be collected and administered by Outlook Express in the same way as a standard mail account. You can also perform the process if you already have a Hotmail address.

Q **Is it possible to retrieve email messages that have been deleted from the Deleted Items folder in Outlook Express?**

A The Recover mode of the free DBXtract program (*www.oehelp.com/DBXtract/Default.aspx*) can retrieve messages that have been removed from the Deleted folder, although images and other attachments will probably be lost. Do read the instructions carefully. A friendlier alternative is the new £25 Search and Recover program from Iolo (*www.iolo.com/sr/index.cfm*). It promises to recover almost anything from your hard drive as long as you act quickly.

Q Is there a free email service that is reliable and compatible with both Apple Macs and PCs?

A The best place to start is *www.emailaddresses.com/*, which lists a huge selection of email services, free and paid for. Note that most free services offer only 2MB–3MB of storage space, although Gmail from Google (*www.gmail.com*) provides a whopping 1GB free as long as you put up with advertising inside your messages. Free services worth evaluating are the elegantly styled offering at *www.postmaster.co.uk/* or the groovy Windows only Oddpost service at *www.oddpost.com*.

Q **I run a small business and have heard that sending unsolicited marketing email is now illegal under EU rules. Does that mean I can no longer advertise in this way?**

Sending emails or text messages to any individual is illegal unless the person has chosen to receive them. Unsolicited emails may still be sent to companies as long as there is a clear opt-out clause. Information can be sent to individuals if the recipient has already bought similar products or services from you and has not opted out when previously given the chance. In every message sent, be sure to give clear instructions on how people can contact your company to opt out. For more detailed advice, visit *www.informationcommissioner.gov.uk/eventual.aspx?id=35*.

Q **All the digital photos I send via email are enormous when opened. How can I get round this?**

A Windows XP users have a snazzy function that can solve this problem. Simply click on the photograph's file name with the right-hand mouse button and select Send To – Mail

Recipient. Then tick the 'make all my pictures smaller' box and continue. Other Windows users can try a simple image resizing program such as the £6 EasyImage Lite (*www.chameleon-systems.com/EasyImageLite.asp*) or a free photo-editing program such as AutoSize (*www.btinternet.com/~AnthonyJ/projects/AutoSize/*) or Image Enhance (*http://biphome.spray.se/baxtrom*).

Once you have resized the image, simply attach it to your email in the normal way and send. An interesting alternative is the SendPhotos program (£13 from *www.novatix.com/Products/SendPhotos*).

Q **I have been trying to email a scanned JPEG photo to a Mac-using friend in the US but she is not able to view it. Is there anything I can do from this end or does she need some particular software?**

A She will need to have image viewing software to access the file, but most modern web browsers will handle JPEGs with ease by default. There could also be a problem with the JPEG itself. Try sending another file to see if she gets the same error.

If you get really stuck you can always set up an online album and upload the image file to a specialist photo site such as Shutterfly (*www.shutterfly.com*) or Fotopic (*http://fotopic.net/*). Once you do this your friend can log on and view it privately at her leisure. These are also great places to publish those intimately embarrassing episodes in your life to the whole world, which is, bizarrely, what a lot of people seem to use them for.

Q Are contractual negotiations conducted via email and word processed documents as safe as doing things the conventional way with letters, phone calls and personal visits?

A The basic concept is that a contract is a contract and a document is a document whether on parchment or the side of a cow. It's still early days to talk confidently about the legitimacy of email and digital signing, but many more forward-thinking companies are now happy to conduct negotiations via email and use faxed contracts for the actual signing process. I do, however, recommend you obtain some proper legal advice if you are in any way worried about your particular situation.

Q I started to receive spam email within hours of setting up a brand new Yahoo! email account. How can this be?

A I asked Yahoo! and it was mystified. It's possible your new address was harvested from the Yahoo! Members directory if you opted for a listing. Funnily enough, my public email account at the rival *www.hotmail.com/* receives almost no spam since I went to the Options page and set my Junk Mail Filter to Enhanced.

Q I am receiving pornographic emails, even though I have never visited any suspect websites. Could they be triggered by information on my own website?

A Make sure you have not placed your email address on your website in an easily readable format. This is because spam and porn purveyors send out robot scavenger programs to collect email addresses from sites to sell on or exploit. If you do have a contact email address, disguise it by writing it out as 'name at address dot com' or encrypt it with the free Mail Coder program available at *www.farook.org.*

Q I run a monthly email newsletter, but my current Yahoo! service is not very good. Can you recommend an alternative?

A I like the MailerMailer service at *www.mailermailer.com/*, which provides newsletter mailing services ranging from 200 mailings a month for free up to 500,000 a month for £200 (at which level, I suggest, it is time to prune your address list). An international service, it offers free templates, automatic email address validation and mailout scheduling to manage your mailing service efficiently.

Alternatively, visit *www.infacta.com/* and download the Group Mail Free program. This free delivery software will set up automated and personalised email newsletters, as well as handling subscriptions, messages that bounce back and all

the other paraphernalia required by your average email
publishing magnate. There are a few limitations with the free
version, but you can always upgrade to a fully featured paid-
for one (from £50) as your needs grow.

Q **Outlook Express logs me off every time I send an email. Can
I stop this happening?**

A Fire up Outlook Express and go to the Tools – Options –
Connection Setting, then uncheck the box that says 'Hang up
after sending and receiving'. Bingo. Those suffering from
random disconnections should try opening up Internet
Explorer, going to Tools – Options – Connections – Settings
and on the Advanced button, uncheck the box that says,
'Disconnect if idle'. If you do this, make sure you close your
connection manually after each session.

Q **Is there a simple way to transfer my entire email Outlook
Express book and messages from one computer to another?**

A Later versions of Outlook Express will export your
address book to either a standard text format or a file that can
be imported and read by Outlook Express on another
machine. Select File – Export – Address Book then follow
the prompts. Alternatively, try downloading the excellent £22
Express Assist from *www.ajsystems.com/* (a free trial is

available on the site) to create an automatic back-up of all emails, address books and a host of other bits and pieces. It's one of my favourite utilities and well worth the price.

Q **My computer continually fails to download a large email attachment, blocking all subsequent messages. How can I clear this?**

A Visit a web email service such as Mail2web (*www.mail2web.com/*) and connect to your email service from there. Locate the offending message, then delete it. Be careful, though – once deleted, it is gone for good.

Q **Why do some of my email messages sent to AOL addresses get through, while others seem to disappear?**

A AOL has a reputation as an eccentric, and some would say Machiavellian, email service. Lost attachments, disappearing messages and other strange phenomena are apparently regular occurrences. Some of this is simply down to the old-fashioned nature of the AOL machine. For example, files larger than 2MB cannot be sent to an AOL customer from outside the system, and the company's email software is very fussy about accepting HTML-formatted messages.

Nowadays, most lost mail is the result of AOL spam filters being overzealous when rejecting suspect mailheaders

and the like. Read the dropped mail FAQ page at
http://members.aol.com/adamkb/aol/mailfaq/dropped-mail.html or AOL's own mail information page at
http://postmaster.info.aol.com/ for a list of common causes
and cures. As a last resort, contact AOL directly at
postmaster@aol.com, with a fully documented account of
your problems.

Q **I have received an email request from my online bank to
send details of my password and account to update their
records. Is this genuine?**

A Beware of email messages that ask for anything private
to do with online financial activities. It does not matter how
official they look, with company logos and addresses that
appear to come from the right place: they are a scam.
Nationwide and Halifax customers were targeted recently by
the fraudsters, but no bank or financial institution will ever
email you to ask for these details, so do not divulge them.
Immediately notify the organisation concerned about the
approach to help it catch those involved.

Q **Are there programs that will convert my Outlook address
book into indexed Filofax pages?**

A Addresses can be conveniently de-digitised with the

£12.50 Address Book Software (available by download from
www.filofax.co.uk/. Once installed, you can export your
Outlook data as a CSV file (click on File – Export – Address
Book then follow the instructions) and import the addresses
into the Filofax software, ready for printing out onto the
company's paper.

Q **Whenever I open Outlook Express it operates very slowly.
I regularly defrag my hard disc and empty temporary internet
folders, so what could be the problem?**

A Outlook Express is very fussy about how untidy the
message folders are, so every so often you need to don your
apron and do a bit of housekeeping. Open Outlook Express
and select the Local Folders tab on the left-hand side of the
screen. Then click on File – Work Offline and once you have
done that go to File – Folder – Compact All Folders. This
compression and tidy up process may take a few minutes
depending on the number of messages you have stored, after
which you can switch back to an online mode which will
hopefully feel much snappier.

Q **Can I set up an automatic response in Outlook Express to
reply to my emails when I am out of the office?**

A Most large companies have auto responders built into their email system, but small firms or individuals who want this facility need to have a permanent broadband connection to the internet – rather than just a dial-up service – and must keep their computer and email package running while they're away.

You can set up an auto-reply system using the Message Rules feature under Tools in Outlook Express. For a detailed animated tutorial of the process go to *http://visualtutorials.com/email.htm*, or for a professional fee-based responder service visit *www.auto-responder.co.uk/*.

Bear in mind, though, that you are likely to be replying to spam messages and virus attacks in your absence, which will only confirm that your email address is live, so I would not recommend using auto-response services in this way.

Q How can I make my email messages look more professional?

A As long as you are sure your recipients are happy receiving rich format HTML messages, and you are using a later version of Outlook Express, you can easily create some stationery to replace that boring old black text on a white background. For detailed tutorials on how to use stationery on the different Outlook Express versions visit *http://thundercloud.net/help/*.

A more receiver-friendly alternative is simply to add a professional looking signature at the end of every email. Go to Tools – Options – Signatures and create your own default signature by clicking on New. You can find more detailed instructions at *http://email.about.com/cs/oetipstricks/qt/et112703.htm.*

Q How can I move addresses from my address book in Outlook Express into Hotmail?

A If you are using a later version of Outlook Express and have added your Hotmail account to OE, click Tools – Address Book then select Tools – Synchronize Now. This will synchronise your Outlook Express WAB (Windows address book) with the contacts stored in your Hotmail address book. You must, of course, be online when you do this and do make sure you have at least one address in your Hotmail address book, otherwise it may sync to zero in both books, which is not a happy event.

Q When I scan a document for emailing the resulting JPEG image file is huge. Is there anything I can do to make it smaller?

A The compressed JPEG file format was designed to provide an efficient way of storing and manipulating images on computers, and as such works very well. Nowadays, however, the demands of web and email transmission make it even more important that picture files are as small as possible.

To optimise your image files try *www.spinwave.com/crunchers.html*. It offers a neat free service called JPEG Cruncher which will compress and optimise your images immediately online. If you want more personal control over the process you can download its $49.95 JPEG Cruncher Pro software product for Windows or Macintosh. The company also offers the same service for GIF files.

Q I have never been able to receive attachments correctly. They always appear as dozens of pages of indecipherable symbols – oblongs, squares etc. Is there anything I can do about this?

A This is a common problem, especially for AOL users. File attachments, especially large ones, are commonly transmitted across the internet in a computer friendly encoded format, the three most common of which are Mime, uuencode and BinHex. The encoding and decoding is normally done automatically and we simply receive the full file, but if your email software cannot cope with a particular format it will display the file in its 'raw' state. You need to save the attachment as a file (File – Save As) and download a decoder such as Winzip from *www.winzip.com* to open and decode it. For more information go to *www.winzip.com/uuencode.htm*.

Q Will I be protected from potential virus attacks in email attachments if I use a web-based email service?

A Although web-based mail messages can carry viruses, because the message is being read on a remote computer it should not be able to infect you unless you download and save the mail to your PC. Many web-based services also provide online virus checkers to help prevent the spread of malicious code. My general advice is to be prudent without being paranoid. Keep your home PC virus checker up to date and don't open an attachment unless you know its pedigree, no matter where it's located.

Q Why does it take so long for me to receive email messages sent by friends and business colleagues? Isn't email instant?

A Email messages generally travel around the globe almost instantaneously. I know this because I frequently send messages with attachments to friends in California while speaking on the phone to them and they are received within seconds of my posting. I suggest you consider changing your internet service provider if your experience is different, as this is almost certainly a problem at its end. Occasionally, the system will break down and cause a delay, but that should be the exception rather than the rule.

Q How do I deal with junk email which sends me straight to a website and then prevents me from logging off unless I switch off my computer?

A Junk message that take over your machine, so to speak, are particularly nasty. One way to deal with them is to press the Alt key (next to the space bar) and the F4 button simultaneously to close the open window. You can also cycle out of it by pressing the Alt and Tab keys (next to the Q) together. To delete them from the mail inbox, right mouse click on the message after getting back to your mail reader and click on delete. This is one type of email that, in my opinion, needs to be made illegal.

Q Is it possible to cancel a particularly long incoming email that is taking an unacceptable time to download and carry on receiving the remainder of messages?

A Your best bet is to set up an email rule (Tools – Message Rules) which refuses to download email over a certain size. Make sure you set a size which is large enough to cope with everyday attachments. To check mail before downloading use something like *www.mail2web.com* to view your messages online or the free Pop3 Scan Mailbox software at *www.kempston.net/smb/index.html*.

Q I am worried about the rash of email and website-based computer viruses. Can you recommend reliable anti-virus software that will cope with them?

A Strangely enough, as I was reading your question I received a message containing a particularly unpleasant virus. Luckily, I have a couple of rotweiller packages which seem to do their job well. First line of defence is the free anti-virus package AVG from *www.grisoft.com* which copes nicely with known virus types and has an efficient update procedure. I back this up with the $29.95 MailDefense from *www.indefense.com*, which stops dead any malicious scripts and other email nasties from entering or leaving your email system.

Q I have 200 emails stored in Outlook Express that I want to transfer into a document for editing. Can I do this en bloc rather than individually?

A If you are using Outlook Express 6.0, which is the latest version, try using the combine and decode function which is actually designed for decoding multi-part messages. Highlight and select the messages you want to transfer and then click on Message – Combine and Decode, and click OK. The program will combine all the message texts into one large message which you can save as a text file or cut and paste into any word processing package. For something a little more sophisticated check out the powerful email tools in Mailbag Assistant at *www.fookes.com/mailbag/*

Q How can I change the default font on Outlook Express? At the moment these changes have to be done manually each time an email is sent.

A Tools – Options – Compose. Select the font and size you need and voila. You can also set default sign offs for your email under the Options – Signature settings. Compose a few, set your basic one as the default and keep a couple of alternatives which you can select from the Insert menu option when writing a new message.

Q **I recently tried to send an e-card to a friend but it was rejected because it was an 'executable attachment'. What does this mean?**

A Your innocent e-card has been nobbled by a covert branch of the internet police, I'm afraid. Most internet service providers now have anti-virus technology which bounces back any message it believes may contain a virus attachment. Your card looked suspicious because it was an executable attachment, which means you get it to work simply by clicking on it when it arrives in your inbox. Next time, compress the file using something like the free FilZip (*www.filzip.com/en/index.html*) before sending and it should arrive with no problems.

Q **I was recently struck by a computer virus, which I managed to clean out eventually. How can I let my whole address book know and warn them?**

A I'm not sure contacting your whole address book is the best thing to do in this instance, especially if you have a large list of contacts. Instead, check your Sent Items folder in Outlook Express to see who was attacked as a result of your infection and inform them.

Q I usually compose email using Hotmail and don't like to hog our shared telephone/fax line for too long. How can I work off-line?

A The simplest way to pen your eloquent prose is to use a word processing package such as Word, or WordPad which comes free with Windows, and when you've finished select the text with the mouse and click Edit – Copy. You can then fire up your internet connection, go to Hotmail – Compose and right mouse click in the text box to paste your text in without having to type it. If you write several emails before going online, you can then copy and paste them all in a sequence, but make sure you attach the right text to each address.

Q Recently I have been receiving email messages which appear to be web pages. How do you do this, as I would like to send out my newsletter in the same form?

A For those using later versions of Outlook Express simply go to Tools – Options – Send – Mail Sending Format and select HTML. Click OK to save the settings and from that point on all your emails will go out as HTML rather than text. You will need to write and layout your messages as HTML in order to gain the design benefits, and do remember that not everyone can read HTML email by default, so check first with your target readership.

Q **I often use the computer in my local library to check email. How can I prevent other users reading my mail later after I've left?**

A Make sure you log off your internet mail account before you leave the computer, which will prevent subsequent access without a password. Alternatively, try loitering conspicuously while humming to yourself to scare off potential snoopers.

Q **I often receive emails with photo attachments spread over several pages. How can I re-configure them to print onto one sheet of A4 paper?**

A First save the attachment as a JPEG file (File – Save Attachments) then print it out using a photo editing software package rather than from within your email program. In this way you can resize the image to your heart's content. If you don't have an editing package, download the freeware product 20/20 from *www.hotfreeware.com/*.

Q Is it possible to print out my email address book without having to type all the entries out address for address?

A Most good quality email packages include address book printing functions. In Outlook Express, for instance, select Tools – Address Book and click on the print icon (or go to File – Print). This will allow you to print your address book in three different layouts: memo, business card and phone list. Choose the one you want and press OK and you will receive a paper version of your names and addresses. Unfortunately, there is no Little Black Book option with the software as yet, so you will have to bind it yourself.

Q An email of mine is currently on open display on a website which no longer appears to be maintained. Am I doomed to have it there forever or is there a way to get it removed?

A If you have not given permission for it to be displayed, you have every right to have it removed or masked. If the site is not being maintained, contact the owner of the web server and ask them to remove the material. Look up the details via a Whois query at *www.betterwhois.com*. If the owner and poster are the same person, you may have a problem, although if you feel strongly enough it might be worth taking legal advice.

Q Why are a small percentage of people unable to receive my emails when sent in HTML format?

A Not everyone uses HTML enabled email reading software, especially those running older PCs or non Windows machines. The problem is not that the mail fails to get through, it is that it arrives unformatted. It is safest to send email as plain text until you are fairly certain the majority of recipients have HTML enabled readers. By then we will also probably be contending with voice and video mail messages, which will call for a whole new set of rules.

Q I have a very cumbersome email address. Can I create a new one myself?

A Unfortunately, using the default one allocated to you by your internet service provider puts you somewhat at their mercy. You are also, of course, at liberty to go online and sign up for a free web-based email address, and there are plenty to choose from. The largest services of this type are to be found at *www.yahoo.com* and *www.hotmail.com*.

You can also consider registering your own domain name, which will give you an email address of your choice providing the name is available. You can find out more at *www.freeparking.co.uk*. A key point in choosing an email address is that it should be something you can live comfortably with for a long time, because changing your address regularly on a whim will do nothing to enhance your social or business life.

Q Is there any way to ensure that email, laid out in letter format, is received by the addressee in a like manner without the formatting all askew?

A The formatting of email messages is as much a matter for the recipient as the sender. The latter can help by keeping their word wrap to 65 or less, but after that fonts and other

factors pay their part. For a nice utility to tidy up mail, take a look at Message Cleaner from Roundhill Software. This £5 shareware package will format mail and newsgroup messages as well as strip out things like those annoying > marks you get when email is forwarded. It is well worth the registration fee if you're a neat notes person. For more information go to *www.roundhillsoftware.com*.

Q I believe that in order to set up my email facility I need to enter my SMTP and POP3 server details. Can you explain what these terms mean?

A The SMTP (Send Mail Transport Protocol) and POP3 (Points of Presence) servers are the computers which control and transmit the email traffic around the internet, from computer to computer and country to country. They act as the email traffic cops, if you like. SMTP handles your outgoing mail and POP3 your incoming messages. The conventional method of identifying them is using a simple format which includes the name of your ISP. So for instance if your ISP's address is *www.isp.co.uk*, it is likely the SMTP address will be something like *smtp.isp.co.uk* (or sometimes *mail.isp.co.uk*) and the POP3 server address will be pop3.isp.co.uk. However these rules are not sacrosanct, so it is advisable to ask for details from your ISP.

Q When I write a long email on Hotmail and then try to send it, I find I've been disconnected with no advance warning, so all my work is wasted. What is going on?

A Check first that you are not being kicked off by call waiting if you have it enabled. If not, you are probably being disconnected by your internet service provider. All ISPs have an automatic cut off if they do not detect any activity across your connection. This even applies to flat-rate 'anytime' services.

The best way round this is to write your Hotmail messages in a word processing package before you go online, log on and then copy the text and paste it into the Hotmail box using the Edit – Paste function in your browser. It's fast, efficient and gives you plenty of time to compose offline in peace.

Q I am sometimes concerned that my emails are not actually arriving properly. Is there a way of obtaining a receipt showing an email has been received by the addressee?

A If you are using a later version of Windows Outlook Express go to Tools – Options – Receipts and check the Request a Read Receipt box. Those who are super anxious about important emails can use something like the free Registered Email service at *www.registeredemail.com/*, which will allow you to send and track important messages using its specialised server.

3 · Using the internet

The internet is a massive new information and communication channel. That means there are lots of issues, questions and problems you can face when trying to access it.

Getting on to the internet can involve hours of setting up connections, checking passwords and generally fiddling around. The good news is that things are getting better. Modern software systems such as Windows XP, with its super friendly modem set-up routines, do help, as do the simple set-up routines of today's more helpful internet service providers. Even so, the process can involve more than its fair share of hair tugging, so it's small wonder that companies like AOL, with their automatic sign-on CDs which continually seem to pop through the letterbox, make money.

For some, there is also a bit of confusion between the definitions of the internet and the world wide web. The internet is the plumbing; the cabling infrastructure, technology systems and standards that allow for international data communication between computers. The world wide web is a massive collection of 'pages' of information – more than five billion at the last count – which uses the internet as its transport mechanism. To all intents and purposes they are fused inextricably, but it still pays to remember the subtle differences.

The secret to getting the most out of the internet (or the world wide web) is not to be intimidated by the sheer scale of all this information. Just as in a large library, stick to searching for stuff you're interested in and you are likely to find exactly what you need. The internet isn't perfect – the search function needs a lot of work before it will become truly intuitive – but things are getting better all the time.

Top Don't Panic internet tips

Improve your line

Unless you're one of the fortunate early users of a high speed, always-on broadband internet service, you may, at some time or another, have bemoaned the sluggish speed of access to your favourite sites. The causes can be myriad, but one of the most common is a dodgy telephone line. Your wiring may be old, your extension cable too long or you may simply have too many devices, such as fax machines, hanging on the line. Try installing a short, dedicated line with fresh cabling and see if that improves the situation. If all else fails, ask your telephone provider to test the line to see if it needs to be improved or if the 'gain' (volume) should be turned up.

Have a back-up browser

Contrary to what you may believe, Microsoft's Internet Explorer is not the only web browser out there. Download a spare one such as Opera (*www.opera.com*) for use in emergencies in case Internet Explorer stops working. It can save time and heartache later on.

Get a second ISP

Even the best internet service providers go through bad

patches, so it pays to have a spare one ready in case you need to log on in a hurry and your usual ISP won't co-operate. There are plenty of pay-as-you-go services around but my favourite is Freewire (*www.freewire.net*), if only for the simplicity of its access: no passwords, no log-in name, just a phone number. Set it up, test it out to make sure it works and keep the number handy, just in case.

Keep searches specific

Don't be intimidated by search engines; they are your best friend. The key to using them is to make your queries as precise as possible. Be pedantic; if you want Hartleys Lemon Curd, put that into the search box, rather than just Hartleys or curd. You can then widen your search terms if nothing useful comes up. And remember, Google is not the only search service. Try *www.queryster.com* for a great selection of alternative search tools.

Top Don't Panic internet questions

Q Where can I get a complete list of ISPs that will give me internet access and email facilities, and is there any way to access the web without one?

A Internet service providers make the essential link between your computer and those of the internet. You need one to access the web, in the same way you need a telephone company if you want to make a phone call. To get a fairly comprehensive list of ISPs in the UK visit *www.ispreview.co.uk* and check out its reader-generated UK ISP top 20. It's an excellent resource for ISP shoppers and contains lots of useful information which can help you make your choice.

Q I am studying Japanese and would like to access broadcasts in the language to improve my skills. Can you suggest any online services?

A Visit the internet television page at *http://wwitv.com/portal.htm*. The site has a huge selection of streamed television from more than 100 countries, from Azerbaijan to Zimbabwe. The site requires RealPlayer (*www.real.com/*) or Windows Media Player, and a fast broadband connection will obviously improve the quality of the pictures. Sayonara and gambatte.

Q Can you explain to a silver surfer what the different endings on website addresses, such as .org. and .net mean?

A These suffixes are the internet equivalent of postal addresses, but with some subtle differences. Each country has its own – .uk for the UK, .de for Germany and so on – and there are also various generic designators associated with each address. A .co or .com should indicate a commercial entity, .org a non-profit organisation and .net an internet specific group. In fact, it's a bit of a muddle, with suffixes used in all sorts of random ways by people who want a good name for their website and are prepared to pay the licence fees. For an overview of the situation visit *www.learnthenet.com/english/html/84domain.htm.*

Q I surf the net occasionally with a pay-as-you-go service. The connection is terrible and sometimes I have to reconnect 20 times in a session. Is this normal?

A Many of the pay-as-you-go internet services – where you pay only for an 0845 phone call – are notoriously flaky. They cut off without warning, can be sluggish at peak times and generally make surfing as much fun as kissing a bullfrog.

Visit *www.ispreview.co.uk/* and test a selection of the services rated as very fast, although even these may have problems. Otherwise, consider paying a little extra for a monthly subscription service.

Q **Is it possible to use my ISP service on both my laptop computer and new desktop PC without having to sign up again?**

A You do not have to sign up twice with your internet service provider for different machines. Simply enter the details of your existing account into the internet sign-up wizard (Start – Programs – Accessories – Communications) in Windows 98 or XP and you can connect as normal. You will also need to enter information relating to your email account servers, so check your ISP sign-up documents for this before you start. However, I recommend you use only one of the computers to collect your email otherwise things can become very confusing.

Q **I am looking to sell my house online. Do you have any suggestion about how to do this without setting up a website?**

A The pounding you hear in the distance is a horde of wild-eyed estate agents stampeding up your path, online sales brochures aflutter. Try this simple test – go to *www.google.co.uk* and enter 'house for sale UK'. I got

3.4 million results. To save your sanity, a combination of the quirky service at *www.just-a-sign.com* coupled with *www.agentfreesales.co.uk* could fit your bill.

Q **How can I stop my dial-up connection box popping up inconveniently while I am performing other tasks on the PC like playing games? It is infuriating.**

A Have you, perchance, set your email program to check for mail at regular intervals? If so this could be the reason for the interruptions. Alternatively, check if you have any programs running which use the built-in task scheduler to try to automatically access the internet for updates. Do this by double clicking the Scheduler icon in the task bar at the bottom of the screen to see if anything shows up in the Scheduled Task box.

You may have to resort to setting the 'Never dial a connection' feature within Internet Explorer (Tools – Internet Options – Connections) to stop the problem, which will take away the convenience of the PC dialling your ISP automatically every time you fire up the browser. Nowadays you may also be the victim of a rogue dialler program which is trying to phone out to cause mayhem with your machine. Download a good anti-Trojan program such as AdAware from *www.lavasoftusa.com* and see if it can locate anything.

Q **My internet browser's start page has been hijacked to display another site. When I change it back it returns after an hour or so. What can I do?**

A Pop along to *www.pjwalczak.com/spguard/* and download Piotr Walczak's free StartPage Guard. This clever little program will detect and prevent attempts to change your start page, removing most intruders that it finds. The program also protects your favourite search-page settings.

Q **I am a student. Is there any way I can use my computer to communicate with other students without having to pay call charges?**

A There are a growing number of communication software packages which allow you to chat with friends using the internet rather than the telephone. The drawback is both parties must be online and using the same software, along with a machine which has a microphone and speakers. If you fit the bill, try the PalTalk service from *www.paltalk.com/PalTalkSite/products.html*. This lets you chat away with video or audio to any other PalTalk subscriber for free.

Q **What is the cheapest way to access the internet when I'm abroad?**

A AOL users can connect via the many local access numbers available to subscribers worldwide, although there will be a surcharge for using the service internationally. Check with *www.aol.co.uk* for details or use keyword Global. For others the best bet is probably to use the joint iPass/i2roam service (*www.i2roam.com*). It will cost around $4.99 a month plus 12¢ a minute in Europe, but for frequent business travellers it could still work out cheaper than hotel international phone rates. It's also worth checking out the Net2Roam service from *www.net2roam.com*.

Q We hear a lot about cookies, but aren't IP addresses a bigger threat to privacy and security?

A An IP address is the numeric identifier (eg 21.212.129.123) of a specific computer on a network or internet connection. They are not so much a threat as a necessity, as they make sure your data moves safely back and forth across the internet and that you can access the website you are aiming for. The real danger comes if you switch on your computer's file and printer sharing without having a firewall in place to block unauthorised entry by someone sinister. Helpful advice on the whole internet security and privacy issue can be found at *http://grc.com/x/ne.dll?bh0bkyd2*.

Q Why does my PC keep disconnecting from the internet for no apparent reason?

A There can be any number of reasons for these annoying disconnections. Ensure call waiting has been disabled. For the majority of phone companies, dial *43# on your phone to do this, and #43# to enable it again afterwards. Alternatively, you may have a particularly bad phone line which is causing the modem to lose the signal. You could try asking your telephone provider to turn up the gain (or volume). Some internet providers also specify that the connection will be broken if there is no discernible activity for a number of minutes, so try not to doze off.

Q Are there any websites that can help me identify some music that is on my mind and driving me mad?

A Visit Melodyhound at *www.name-this-tune.com*. The site offers an innovative melody finder that determines tunes whistled into a computer's microphone. It sounds weird but it worked for me with Beethoven's Fifth. Avoid trying this at work, however, unless you want funny looks from your colleagues. For a slightly different take on identifying modern hits, try the Shazam mobile phone service at *www.shazam.com*.

Q **I recently downloaded a freeware software program and am now receiving much more spam. Is there a connection?**

A I suspect it is just a coincidence. If you did not provide your email address as part of the download process, you should be safe. Most shareware and freeware software authors are scrupulously careful in hiding their transactions from spammers. If a program or website ever asks for an email address without good reason, hand over a disposable address from a free anti-spam service such as *www.spamgourmet.com* or *www.spamhole.com*.

Q **When I mistype web addresses in Internet Explorer, I am redirected to the MSN search site. Can I change this to Google?**

A The Googlify your browser page, *www.google.com/options/defaults.html* provides tools for the world's most popular search engine. Google can be set as your home page and default search engine, though I am still waiting for the button to request that Google personnel come round and make the tea while I wait for a search to finish. Internet Explorer's search feature can be turned off by selecting Tools – Internet Options – Advanced – Search from Address Bar and picking the Do Not Search option.

Q **I currently have an ISDN line to connect to the internet. Should I consider changing to broadband?**

A It really depends on how much time you spend online. If you plan to do much more surfing and internet work, broadband has the advantage of always being on and, unlike ISDN, there is no dial-up charge, only a flat monthly fee. Broadband services are also faster, which can make it easier to transfer files. There are lots of good deals on broadband access nowadays. Take a look at *www.adslguide.org.uk* for a selection.

Q **When I listen to internet radio on my computer, the sound keeps stuttering. Should I change my software?**

A Your problem probably has more to do with your internet connection than the player software. Check that no other internet programs, such as email, are running at the same time and that your internet connection generally runs at close to its rated speed (usually around 40kbps on a 56K modem). Also, try downloading the free Winamp player at *www.winamp.com* to see if that works any better. By the way, I recently stumbled across a great site at *www.publicradiofan.com*. This is a wide-ranging resource for all kinds of world radio stations.

Q At long last, my area is about to become broadband-enabled, but I am confused by the large number of suppliers available. Is there a site that can give advice?

A A great site for this kind of information is Rowland O'Connor's Broadband Help at *www.broadband-help.com*. It provides a wealth of advice and customer recommendations on all types of broadband, including cable and satellite services. The internet provider reviews are especially helpful – check the user-ratings column to locate companies that offer a good service as well as competitive prices.

Q Whenever I print text from a website, the right-hand edge is missing. How can I correct this?

A Strange web designs often cause this – sites with badly coded frames or extra wide pages, for example. Try printing in landscape mode (found in printer preferences under the Print menu). If that doesn't work, click on File – Page Setup in Internet Explorer, clear the headers and footers and set the left and right margins to 0.5mm. Alternatively, cut and paste the text into your word processing software and print from there. There are reports that this is actually a bug in Internet Explorer's browser which can be cured by setting the fonts display to Large Fonts (View – Text Size) but I haven't been able to confirm this yet.

Q Will the speed at which I can connect to the internet vary with different service providers?

A Definitely. Good ISPs will ensure they have an optimal set up for the number of customers they have, while others may restrict the bandwidth or modem ports available for subscribers, impairing connect speeds. This can sometimes be indicated by a marked slow down in surfing speeds in the evening, as a lot of people get home and log on to a congested service to browse and access their email. However, other factors, such as the quality of your modem, do play a part. If you generally connect at speeds above 48kbps, be thankful.

Q **Is it possible to listen to BBC radio services over the internet in northern Italy?**

A The Beeb has a fabulous online radio service at *www.bbc.co.uk/radio*, offering audio feeds of broadcasts by everyone from John Peel to Sir Andrew Davis. Those on a dial-up connection should turn off all the slow-loading graphics by clicking the Text Only button at the top left of the page, then select the Listen To links. For a comprehensive set of links to live feeds of all British radio stations, visit *www.radiofeeds.co.uk*. Your internet connection will need to be left running during webcasts.

Q **I recently received a huge phone bill and have been told that it is because my computer was hijacked by a 'rogue dialler'. How can I prevent this happening again?**

Rogue dialler programs load onto your computer after you access a website and unwittingly agree to some small print. They then redirect internet connection calls to expensive premium rate numbers. The first you know about it is when a bill for hundreds of pounds arrives. Take care when agreeing to any suspicious downloads from sites and read onscreen small print carefully. A dial-up protection program called DialGuard can be downloaded from *www.stormloader.com/dialguard*, while a useful list for identifying premium-rate numbers can be found at *www.icstis.org.uk/icstis2002/PhoneNumberLookup/AskPhone Number.asp*.

Q I keep hearing about rich media, but what does it mean?

A Rich media, otherwise known as multimedia, refers to any data incorporating graphic, animated and/or audio components, so adding to the 'richness' of the basic text. *The Sunday Times*'s CD ROM The Month or DVD ROM titles and websites such as encyclopedias are the main producers of this type of material. Visit *www.encarta.com* for a good example.

Q My parents refuse to use their credit card over the internet. Is there any other means of buying goods online?

A The credit card companies are looking to introduce a sort of pay-as-you-go card in the UK sometime soon, which should alleviate most people's fears. In the meantime, the nearest thing to a prepay voucher for e-shopping is the Splash Plastic card (*www.splashplastic.com*), though it suffers from limited online store support.

Q I have a brilliant idea for a website but am worried about protecting the idea. Can you help?

A The site of the Entrepreneurship Centre at Imperial College (*www.ec.ms.ic.ac.uk*) is a good place to start. It offers sound advice on all aspects of starting a business, from patents and copyright to raising money. The DTI and Patent Office Innovation Logbook service at *www.innovationlogbook.gov.uk* is also worth considering as a way of documenting your idea in a protectable form. Good luck.

Q How can one be sure that buying from an internet retailer is secure?

A I have been buying products online for five years and have avoided problems by following a few basic rules. Buy British if possible – unless you know the company well or are buying software downloads – as it is easier to seek legal redress from a UK site. Avoid sites that do not include a postal address and landline phone number. Always buy on a credit card and never send cash by services such as Western Union to countries with a reputation for fraudulent online activity, such as Romania, the Ukraine and Indonesia. For these use escrow services instead (*www.escrow.com*). If in doubt, don't buy. For further advice, visit *www.consumer.gov.uk/consumer_web/e-shopping.htm*.

Q How can I submit my website to the search engine services to help people find it?

A You are actually asking two questions: how to submit your site and how to improve the odds of someone finding it. Both are answered at
http://searchenginewatch.com/webmasters/index.php.
My advice is to offer genuinely helpful facts and continually refreshed information on your site, which should encourage others to link to you, and contact similar sites to discuss exchanging links. Search engines, particularly Google, love sites that other sites link to. Finally, never forget the power of promoting your site in relevant online discussion groups and forums by including its address in your online signature.

Q How can I store files online so that I can access them from any PC?

A The Yahoo! Briefcase service at
http://briefcase.yahoo.com offers 30MB of free space for files and documents, which you can access from any PC in the world with an internet connection and web browser. You can even share them with Aunt Maude from Bexley if you want, and if you need more space you can upgrade to a fee-paying service. As an alternative try the free Znail service at *http://znail.com/*. It offers only 5MB at the basic

level, but you can increase this to 200MB if you're willing to play its points game and provide a little bit of cash.

Q **I want to register for a broadband service when it comes to our area shortly. Will I be able to keep my pay-as-you-go internet service running?**

A Definitely. Everyone who upgrades to broadband, whether cable or ADSL, should keep a standard dial-up service as a backup. Make sure you don't overwrite the dial-up settings on your computer – you can revert manually by selecting a different connection within Internet Explorer (Tools – Internet Options – Connections). If you don't have dial-up, locate a pay-as-you-go service such as Freewire (*www.freewire.net*) for emergencies. A back-up will let you access email if the fast connection goes wrong, via a service such as the free *www.mail2web.com*.

Q **How do I download music from the internet?**

A Most music tracks available from the internet are stored in MP3 or Windows Media format. To download them, simply go to a music site (you will find a long list on the 'one million free and legal tracks' page at *www.enorgis.com/pmwiki/pmwiki.php*), choose a genre and artist, then right click with your mouse on a track file name or MP3 icon. Choose Save Target As to copy it onto your hard disk. Some sites use a Download button, in which case simply click on it to start the process.

Q **Why don't price-comparison sites such as Kelkoo work? Whenever I click on their links, I cannot find the product listed.**

A Comparison sites work best when you use them directly. If you access them via a search engine such as Google, you can often find the products have changed – or the listing has moved completely, leaving you staring at an irrelevant screen. The secret to sniffing out a bargain online is to have a lot of patience. Use more than one comparison site and search engine, and spend at least a couple of hours investigating and refining your search terms before giving up. One interesting, if rather garish, place to start is *www.madaboutbargains.co.uk*.

Q **Please explain the difference between streaming and downloading files, especially video.**

A Audio and video on the web is stored in standard formats. To access the material, you can either download the whole file to your own computer and play it from the hard disk, or the file can be 'transmitted' to you in a stream which you view 'live' like a radio or TV show, in which case the file does not end up stored on your computer. In both cases, you need a program such as Windows Media Player to play the files.

Q **I am involved with the editorial team of our church magazine, and I wonder if you could suggest any suitable clip art we could download?**

A A great place to locate artwork and illustrations of all kinds is at the Clipart Guide site (*www.clipartguide.com*). Be patient, there's a lot out there and it may take a while to locate the exact illustration you need. Use your browser's built-in search function (Ctrl-F in Internet Explorer) to hunt for key words once you've hit a page full of likely looking clip art files.

Q **I am trying to locate a computer manual for an Amiga A600. Can you suggest where I could try?**

A The rather wonderful *www.instruction-manuals.co.uk/* can help you find manuals for all sorts of products, ranging from boats to dishwashers. It's early days yet so there are still some gaps, but you can post a wanted notice – I managed to locate a manual for my ageing answering machine for £4.50, which was a real bonus. Doing a search on Google for the product model number and the word 'manual' can also pay dividends.

Q Is there a site from which I can download legal documents such as partnership forms, preferably for free?

A A good place to start for all sorts of legal advice and information is *www.compactlaw.co.uk*. It provides material on anything from employment to consumer issues, as well as a good selection of documentation covering all sorts of eventualities. Prices range from £20 to £50-plus per document and there are free advice pages on a range of subjects. The site is busy but well designed and offers a premium rate phone service for those in a hurry.

Q I don't want to get left behind in the new media race and am looking for a good evening course to learn how to design a website. Any suggestions?

A Check out *www.hotcourses.com* for a comprehensive list of courses around the UK – search for web design. Babel Tech (020 7221 1483) in London, for example, seems to offer just what you need, although I was a little perturbed to find no mention of pizza guzzling on the syllabus.

Q Are there any websites that provide drum machine beats like the ones found on a modern digital keyboard?

A Samba over to the rhythm section at *www.synthzone.com/*

drums.htm. This lists all sorts of beats which can be downloaded as samples or midi files, as well as one or two useful tutorials. Also check out the free online drum machine at *www.artopod.com/groovelab/*.

Q **I recently purchased a domain name and email forwarding service from a web company, but the forwarding is not working, despite numerous attempts to have the problem corrected. How can I complain or highlight this malpractice?**

A Commercial dealings done over the internet are subject to exactly the same legal rules as any other transaction. In this case, you made a contract with this company to provide you with something that it is failing to do, so you have full rights in law. You should contact your credit card company immediately and formally complain then seek legal help to obtain redress. The fact that it is on the internet is irrelevant unless the company is not based in the UK, in which case it may be trickier to pursue your claim.

Q **How does one obtain a domain name (.co.uk or .com) and what are the costs?**

A There are two components needed to set up a website. The first is a hosting service that rents out computer space on which to store your web pages (for example, *www.lunarpages.com*). The second part is the domain name, which is the address – such as *www.mysite.co.uk*. Site names can be bought either from a web-hosting service or from a dedicated registration agency such as *www.freeparking.co.uk* or *www.uk2.net*. Fees for the address are annual and can be as low as £10 for two years if it is a .co.uk name. Always read the small print, though.

Q I have found some mystery 0845 phone numbers on my bill which when rung prove to be data lines. Is there any way of identifying the source so we can avoid them in the future?

A It sounds like it could be an internet service provider number which is being triggered by some program. Check all the computers in the house for the number in their Dial Up Networking settings area. Select My Computer – Dial Up Networking then right mouse click any connection names and select Properties. Check if any phone numbers displayed match the one you are seeking. If this fails, ask your phone provider to help you trace the owner.

Q How can we protect our small business from growing levels of online credit card fraud?

A Small firms are vulnerable to fraud, especially those using card approval services, as they do not have direct access to card details. Insist on a mailing address, postcode and phone number on order forms, and be wary of different delivery and billing addresses, or PO boxes. Also watch for large orders from risky areas such as Africa or Eastern Europe.

Q I want to set up an online information service which would make recommendations and share those of its users. Could the site be legally liable in any way if someone follows a suggestion and has a bad experience?

A I strongly suggest you have a chat with a legal professional before starting out, but I suspect the rules are the same online as they are offline. At the very least you should consider posting a prominent disclaimer on the site, laying out the terms on which people use your service and ensuring all your visitors understand the limits of your potential liability.

Q Is there anywhere that I can study web design exclusively on the internet?

A Check out *www.living-it.org.uk*. This service sets out to teach the basics of HTML and web page creation and appears to be quite comprehensive. The course is £75 for 30 hours tuition (free or reduced to qualifying 16–19 year olds or those receiving means-tested benefit). You can also probably get a good idea of design criteria yourself from taking a look at other websites or through buying a simple design program such as Web Studio (*www.webstudio.com/*) which contains templates that you can study.

Q Is there a general purpose directory that groups websites in categories rather than just listing them as with a normal search engine?

A There are indeed a number of such search tools on the internet, the biggest is at *www.yahoo.com*. Here you will find a huge selection of categories covering just about every topic under the sun. You can also find a version of this kind of service run by volunteer contributors at *www.dmoz.org/*.

Q When I finish school I would like to go into the IT business. Can you suggest the best areas to focus on?

A That's a huge question. Just about every part of our working life is touched by IT nowadays, which makes it hard to offer advice on specific sectors. Obviously it's important to get a good basic grounding in computers, the Windows (or even Linux) operating system and various applications such as word processing and spreadsheets. The more adventurous may like to explore additional courses in networking, computer programming (you will find a useful site at *www.codewarrioru.com/CodeWarriorU/*) and important technologies such as XML, Java and .NET.

Q Can you recommend a good website on the subject of small garden design, as I would like to do something interesting with my city plot.

A The BBC site at *www.bbc.co.uk/gardening/design/* has a large selection of hints and tips covering all aspects of design, although it does fail to cover the thorny issue of constant rain and grey skies.

Q Is there a website that can help me find a car number plate I want to buy for personal use?

A For the official cherished registration plate service, log on to *www.dvla-som.co.uk*. If you want to locate an existing plate you will probably be better off with NewReg at *www.newreg.co.uk*. The latter has around 15 million numbers so you may well find something that fits the bill.

Q We would like to take our dog with us to Ireland for a short break but can't find any suitable hotels. Is there any way to locate one online?

A Have a sniff around the selection of pet friendly hotels at *www.travelpets.com*. The site is not perfect – the international selection is a little sparse to say the least – but I'm sure that with some more publicity and recommendations from users, it will turn out to be a popular and useful resource.

Q **Could you give me some tips on how to publish a book online?**

A Xlibris at *www.xlibris.com* offers an innovative book publishing service which appears to go way beyond mere vanity publishing. The site lets you upload your manuscript in Word or another suitable format, after which you can choose a range of services priced from around £300, for a basic book and cover package, to £1,000 for custom designed cover artwork. The best bit is that all of these print-on-demand plans include registration with *Amazon.com* and *Barnes&Noble.com*, so your fans can buy your masterpiece from anywhere in the world. You also retain all the publishing copyrights to your work.

Q **We are planning to move house but have yet to choose where. Is there a website that can assist our search?**

A The best known service of this type is *www.upmystreet.co.uk*, which is superb for gathering information on every aspect of a locality down to the nearest fish and chip shop. My only gripe is that coverage still appears to be limited mostly to towns rather than rural areas. A useful alternative is *www.ukvillages.co.uk*, but this site is very clunky.

Q Where can I locate some old movie stills or black and white photos of the type used on greetings cards today?

A The internet is a movie buffs' paradise and you can locate any number of wonderful photographic material online – at a price. A good place to start is the Internet Movie Database at *www.imdb.com/Sections/Gallery/list*, which has a great selection of posters and photos from several movie generations. Try also *www.hollywoodmegastore.com/moviestills.html* for a reasonably priced collection and, finally, you must visit the Motion Picture and Television Photo Archive at *www.mptv.net/*.

Q I may be moving home later this year. Is there any chance that I can study A levels or the new A/S levels over the internet so as to avoid relocation problems?

A A comprehensive selection of 28 GCSE and A level courses for use at home or via a school is available at *www.samlearning.com*. The Sam@Home online tuition – which costs around £99.95 a year – appears to focus on exam techniques, using multiple choice test and self-assessment sessions as building blocks. I was somewhat underwhelmed by the design of the website but the service seems to have respectable credentials.

Q Can you help me find sound effects for my film projects on the internet?

A Log on to *www.findsounds.com/* which contains a comprehensive listing of all sorts of groovy sounds in a variety of formats, sizes and quality. The best thing about the site is the search facility, which will let you locate anything from a Flipper-like dolphin chitter to the sound of a car door slamming.

Q Why do some American retailers on the web refuse to accept orders from buyers outside the US?

A It all stems from an incident on December 16, 1773 when a group of American patriots threw 342 chests of tea belonging to the British East India Company into Boston Harbour as a protest against a tea tax. From that time on, American stores have been reluctant to deal with people outside the US in case their own products were similarly abused. Alternatively, it could be caused by the fear of potential credit card fraud from untraceable international accounts or an irrational dislike of our friendly VAT men. Whatever the reason, it is one of those mysteries which, like the Bermuda Triangle, is unlikely to be solved anytime soon.

Q I would like to set up my PC to listen to radio stations broadcasting on the internet. How can I do this?

A The set up is pretty straightforward. Simply ensure you have a sound card, speakers and a software player such as RealMedia (*www.real.com*) installed on your PC. A free media player is also included with Windows, although you may need to upgrade if it is an older version (visit *www.microsoft.com/windows/windowsmedia* for more details). Most modern PCs come with these components installed by the way. Once you are all set, visit *www.radio-locator.com* and select a station to try. Be aware, though, that the good old days of advert-free internet radio have long gone.

Q What are 'cookies' and how do I turn them on and off?

A Cookies are small files deposited on your PC by a website that you are visiting. They log your stay and are generally used to provide a more personalised response on your return, such as remembering your log-on preferences so you don't have to enter them again. Cookies have now gained a bad reputation because of the potential to use them to 'spy' on you and detect other places you may have visited on the web. Nevertheless, they can still perform a useful function.

To switch them off in Internet Explorer go to Tools –

Internet Options – Security and set a Custom Level with the cookies box set to disabled. For more detailed information and a list of cookie disabling software visit *www.cookiecentral.com*.

Q Is it possible to install and use a new browser on my machine while retaining the existing one?

A Yes it is. You simply need to install the new browser according to the instructions and start it up from the Program menu or via a desktop shortcut icon. You may get a box asking if you want to make it your default browser – I suggest you say no until you're sure you're ready to change from your present one. There are a number of interesting and useful alternatives to Internet Explorer on the market. Visit *http://dir.yahoo.com/Computers_and_internet/Software/intern et/World_Wide_web/Browsers/* for a comprehensive list.

Q My son plays internet games but suffers from lag, even using a good PC. Is there anything we can do to get over this problem?

A Lag and latency – where the computer stutters heavily during play – is the big enemy of online gaming and can be caused by a slow connection speed, a low specification PC and even the quality of your ISP. Make sure there are no unnecessary programs running in the background when you are playing, keep your video drivers bang up to date and try lowering the graphics quality in the game to improve the frame rate. One good test is to try using a different ISP – such as a free 0845 one like *www.freewire.co.uk* – to see if that helps, as some are simply not geared up for gamers.

Q **Often when I access a website it will display a message saying 'an error has occurred in the script on this page'. What does this mean?**

A Certain websites achieve their fancy effects by using clever programming techniques based around what's known as a scripting language. Errors of the sort you're experiencing may indicate the site's designers have not implemented their programming correctly or that there is a problem with your browser. If you are using an older browser it may help to upgrade, and you should check the scripting feature is switched on in your browser, as it may have been switched off if you are using a high security setting. In Internet Explorer go to Tools – Internet Options – Security and see that Active Scripting is enabled under Custom Settings.

Q **I am looking for a list of quotes but am finding it very difficult to locate the exact thing I am looking for. How can I be more precise in my search terms?**

A With more than a billion pages of information on the web, it can be a real chore to locate your specific information. Always start with the most exact quote you can and put it inside quotation marks, for example 'little red corvette'. This should give you a more precise number of returns, and if they are no good, you can always widen the search by changing the phrase slightly. Also try more than one engine – it pays to search around – and make frequent use of the 'and' and 'near' options. For more detailed information go to *http://searchenginewatch.com/facts/index.html*.

Q Every two hours I get disconnected from the internet by my flat-rate ISP and have to reconnect. How can I stop this happening please?

A You're out of luck I'm afraid. Many of the newer flat-rate internet services impose a mandatory two to four-hour cut off. They claim this is to prevent abuse and that you can immediately redial, but I think they're just being mean. For a list of companies which offer alternatives with no cut off, visit *www.ispreview.co.uk/new/unmetered.shtml*.

Q Can I register with two ISPs? If so how do I switch between them?

A You can register with as many internet service providers as you want, but you will have to set up a profile for each one which will include its phone number and your username and password. You may also need such esoteric information as DNS, POP and SMTP server addresses. Check *www.annoyances.org/win98/features/dun.html* to learn about some of the issues involved with setting up ISPs under Windows ME and 98.

Q I have a website on Geocities and I would like to get a
domain name for it with automatic redirection. Is there a service
you can recommend?

A There are a lot of domain name registration companies in
the UK. Most reputable internet service providers offer the
service and there are also 'boutique' firms such as uk2net
(*www.uk2net.net*) which offer cheap and cheerful 'no support'
services including redirection. Your choice is really down to
the issue of support and reliability balanced against cost.

The cheapest minimal support services cost £5 to £10
a year, while a domain name from someone like NetNames
(*www.netnames.co.uk/*) will cost between £25 and £35 a year.
If you just want a short address and are not fussy about the
name, try the free domain service at *www.freedomain.co.nr/*.

Q Is it possible for members of my family to use a private web
chat room to talk to each other in real time?

A There are a number of ways to establish private
conversations across the internet. The most common is to use
something like Skype (*www.skype.net*) which you can
configure as a private telephone service. Only give out the
contact details to your family so you can have online voice
conferences without others joining in. Another option is to
try one of the websites such as FamilyBuzz

(*www.familybuzz.com*) or Family Moment
(*www.familymoment.com/*) for a complete family web
experience, including online photo albums, gift lists and
message boards.

Q **I have seen some book illustrations on various web pages
and wonder whether I would be in breach of copyright if I linked
directly to these images from my own site?**

A Linking directly (or deep linking) to images which are
on a remote site is now considered to be against the general
policy of the web, since it uses up the bandwidth of the site
you are linking to – which costs it money. There can also be
copyright issues associated with the practice, especially when
it concerns images, so I would suggest you avoid it, or
contact the owners directly to ask for their linking policy
and/or permission. You can find some valuable advice on this
at *www.well.ac.uk/wellclas/copy.html* and at
www.cla.co.uk./copyrightvillage/internet.html.

Q **I keep getting pop-up alerts advertising everything from diet
pills to security programs. How can I stop them?**

A Try Pop-Up Stopper from *www.panicware.com*. The free
version cuts out annoying pop-ups from websites, although
do remember that smaller websites can only operate if we

support them in some way by accessing their adverts. The $29.95 Professional version of the software will also stop pesky ads from MSN Messenger and AOL. Those wanting to rid themselves of Windows Messenger Service spam should download ShootTheMessenger from *http://grc.com/stm/ShootTheMessenger.htm*.

Q I get tired of having to log onto the internet every time I come across a web address I want to keep for future reference. Is there an offline way of collecting these URLs?

A Try Urlybird at *www.somewareonthe.net/urlybird.htm*. It's a small shareware utility ($9.95 to register) that sits in your Windows tray and waits for you to copy a web address into the clipboard. It then allows you to import it at will into your browser of choice. It's very useful for capturing addresses from emails and other documents. Alternatively, there's always paper and pencil!

Q I have recently crafted my first web page and am keen to release it to the waiting public, however I am unsure about the FTP process. Can you help?

A FTP – or file transfer protocol – is the technology used to move your website files from your own PC to the internet server which are to be their home. A good free FTP program is SmartFTP from *www.smartftp.com*, although novices may find it a tad complex. A simpler but more basic program is the free Easy FTP from *www.geocities.com/liquidcoresoftware/easyftp/*.

Q **I frequently listen to net broadcasts using streaming technology. Is there a way of saving these files for later listening?**

A Streaming audio feeds, by definition, are usually designed for listening and not for recording, although some broadcasts do allow it. One solution is to use the $11.95 Total Recorder shareware program which will record streams and other audio sources as required. A free trial version is available from *www.highcriteria.com*. Alternatively, check out the $19.95 Replay Music at *www.replay-music.com*.

Q **How can I enter a pause into a sequence of numbers when setting up the internet service dialling information on my PC?**

A Your Windows PC dialler will recognise commas as pauses when inserted in the correct place. So entering 1,02091231212 will dial 1 then pause for a second before dialling the rest of the number. Each comma represents a second, so if one doesn't do the trick, experiment with two or more to increase the delay. This is handy in an office or hotel where you need to dial 9 for an outside line before connecting.

Q Some sites have very large text on them, how can I change the font so the page fits on one screen?

A In later versions of Internet Explorer go to View – Text Size and choose from the five settings (Smallest to Largest). This will let you juggle the page size to fit your screen more efficiently. Note, it will not work with sites which make use of sophisticated programming techniques to lock their overall design layout.

Q Do you know of a website where one can ask a general question on any subject and receive an answer from any bright spark who logs on?

A The nearest to that concept which I know of is the Google Answers service at *http://answers.google.com/answers/*. You pose your question in one of the set categories, state the price you are willing to pay and an expert researcher will come back with an answer. Obviously much of the benefit of this kind of service depends on the quality of the experts, but Google claims to screen them all to ensure quality. See also the *www.experts-exchange.com* site for IT questions.

Q I am still receiving letters apparently from fan websites of an artist I used to manage some years ago. How can I have my details deleted?

A Try entering 'your name' + 'the name of your artist' in a search engine such as *www.google.com*. From there you should be able to identify the culpable sites and write asking them to delete your details.

Q Can I back up my dial-up network settings? I have three ISPs installed and I would like an easier way to move them to a new computer or restore them after a crash.

A The best way in Windows 98 is to click on My Computer – Dial Up Networking then right click and drag the connection icon to your desktop or another folder. From the pop up menu select Copy Here. This converts your connection to a small DUN file which you can copy and move around at will. To install it on another computer, simply drag the file into your new dial-up networking folder. Note, though, that you will have to change the modem settings for the new machine if it has a different modem.

Q I am really into online gaming but am finding it difficult because of a slow 56K modem. Could you suggest a reasonably priced alternative connection type?

A Several options spring to mind, including a cable modem service from someone like NTL (*www.ntl.com*) if it's available in your area, ADSL from any of the major suppliers such as Freeserve or BT, and the very cheap (£14.99 a month) ADSL service from PlusNet (*www.plus.net*). At last broadband service pricing is starting to come into line with the rest of the world and it's a very good thing.

Q When I try to print out information from the internet, even if I have saved it to disk first, it keeps on missing out sections. Why is this happening?

A You are probably trying to print websites containing frames or segregated graphic elements, both of which will only print individually and not as a page. Some sites overcome this by offering a 'print this page' option, otherwise you will need to select one frame or element at a time and print them separately.

Q I recently loaded one of those free internet connection CD ROMs onto my computer and now my Internet Explorer always loads with its colours and logos. How can I get back to a plain browser?

A Go to *www.snapfiles.com/get/iepers.html* and download the excellent Internet Explorer Personalizer v 3.0. This neat piece of freeware will let you customise the Internet Explorer browser and/or remove all those annoying customised logos and colours to revert to the standard version. My browser now greets me with 'Hi Gorgeous' every time it starts up. So nice for the ego.

Q The safeweb.com service, which I used to prevent snoopers monitoring my web usage, has been discontinued. Do you know of a similar service?

A Check out the new MegaProxy service at *www.megaproxy.com/freesurf/*. This lets you surf the web anonymously. It will also allow you to switch off cookies, adverts and scripting. Also look at the tiny OffbyOne browser from *www.offbyone.com*. It's free, fits onto a single floppy disk and does not store any web cache data on your hard disk.

Q We are building our own website and would like to find a library of copyright-free photographs/images we might use. Can you help?

A The PixelPerfect service at *www.pixelperfectdigital.com/* offers a good selection of photographs and illustrations which can be used for any purpose, without registration or royalty. Check out also the much larger collection of more than 70,000 free user-submitted images at the Stock Xchng (*www.sxc.hu/index.phtml*). It's a fabulous resource, but the site often operates at glacially slow speeds.

Q Is there anywhere I can obtain a .com or .co.uk web domain name for free?

A If you are not fussy about the content of the name, you can sign up for a free web address from someone like Freeservers (*www.freeservers.com*). You won't be able to choose just any name because it only offers 15 options, but you will receive it – and 12MB of web space – for nothing. If you fancy a different kind of address, visit the CO.NR free domain service at *www.freedomain.co.nr/*.

Q I have developed a small website and would like to know how to help cover my costs by running a little advertising on it. Can you help?

A I've had a word with a dotcom refugee friend and he tells me you need a bit of affiliation. He suggests checking out one of the advertising aggregators which offer small websites a chance to run targeted adverts and earn a little cash. You won't get rich unless you count your visitors in the hundreds of thousands, but you may earn enough to cover all or part of your running costs. Visit Commission Junction at *www.cj.com* or *www.tradedoubler.com* for more details.

Q I've recently started using my PC to play games and would like to play against my brother over the internet. Can you recommend a site?

A Two good sites to try out are Microsoft's Game Zone (*http://zone.msn.com*) and *www.uproar.com/*. Both have a great selection of games you can play online, including bridge, cribbage, chess, dominoes and other board and arcade games. You'll need to arrange a time and online room in which to meet, and you may need to register and download a special plug-in, but after that it should be plain sailing. Be warned, though, that online game playing is extremely addictive, so make sure you're sitting down before you open future phone bills.

Q I have decided to set up my own internet radio show. What tools would you recommend for both live and pre-recorded shows?

A I assume you are going to be using either *www.shoutcast.com* or *www.live365.com* as the free host of your show, in which case most of the work will be done for you. You will need a good quality ISP, a reasonable specification multimedia computer and a big enough hard disk – I suggest 20GB minimum – to store any music tracks you will be playing. Make sure you have copyright clearance on all material, use a decent MP3 file manipulator such as the free Winamp (*www.winamp.com*) and you should be fine.

Q I am looking for a reliable, cost-effective internet telephony service provider to make calls to the Caribbean. Can you recommend any?

A Internet telephone services are something of a mixed bag at the moment. There are several on the market, but most have yet to prove there is a sustainable profit waiting at the business end of their dial tone. Two of the steadier ones are *www.net2phone.com* and *www.dialpad.com*, although you may find these PC-to-phone services are losing their price advantage as the offline market catches up. Compare the rates between these sites and conventional phone-to-phone services in the UK such as Onetel (*www.onetel.co.uk*) and Tiscali (*www.tiscali.co.uk/services/smarttalk/*).

Q **Is there any way to eliminate all the peripheral stuff and just print text when printing a web page?**

A Look for the 'printer friendly' button on a lot of websites which when pressed removes all the extraneous material and leaves you with a clean looking text page to print. If there is no button and you are desperate, you can always copy and paste the material from the site into your favourite word processor, after which you can edit it to taste.

Q **I am trying to set up an online community for a small association. Can you recommend any suitable services?**

A I have ploughed my way through most of the major services, including those from MSN Communities at *www.msn.com* and Yahoo's version at *www.yahoo.com* and have yet to find one that is perfect. The new service at *www.communityzero.com*, however, caught my attention recently with its elegant design, simple set up and comprehensive features. The site offers a full range of facilities including instant and email chat, notice boards and calendars.

Q I am a heavy user of the Google search engine. How can I clear out all the redundant and misspelled search terms it seems to remember?

A Actually it's not Google that is remembering your earlier entries, but your browser. If you are using Internet Explorer and have auto-complete switched on, all previously visited online forms will remember your past entries automatically. Disable this feature on later versions of the browser by clicking on Tools – Internet Options – Content – Autocomplete. An explanation can be found at *www.google.com/help/faq.html - ie history.*

Q The internet is spreading rapidly here in Nigeria and while the websites you list in your column are great, access here is still very slow. Can you give some hints on how to make it faster?

A There is no simple cure I'm afraid. You can cheat a little, however, by installing a web browser accelerator which buffers pages so they load faster the next time you visit a site. Go to *www.propel.com* for an example of the type of product I mean. Other than that, your only hope is to petition for an improvement in your internet and phone services as we constantly do with BT and others over here. Good luck!

Q My PC has recently started to refuse to download things from websites. I click on the download button and nothing happens at all. Have I done something wrong somewhere?

A This could be a problem with a corrupt browser. Try re-installing your browser to see if that helps, but if you are desperate click on the file name with the right mouse button and select Save As. You should then be able to force the browser to download the file manually.

Q I am a student with a small web design site and have just received a lawyer's letter from a big company claiming the rights to my .co.uk domain. I can't afford high legal fees so what can I do to protect myself from this bullying?

A Some companies now assume that just because they own a trademark in one country they automatically own the rights to the name everywhere. They don't and as long as you are not a cybersquatter – they register names simply to exploit a legitimate trademark holder – you should be fine. This legal bullying has earned several companies a bad name recently, most notably BAA and even Warner Brothers, who have been employing these heavy-handed tactics against Harry Potter fan sites run by enthusiastic children. Don't panic, instead check out the Domain Name Rights Coalition support site at *www.domainnamerights.org/*.

Q Is there a website giving a list of books which can be downloaded from the net?

A The eBook Directory (*www.ebookdirectory.com*) lists most of the major ebook sites. Project Gutenberg (*http://promo.net/pg/index.html*) is also a great site which contains more than 1,500 free pre-1923 out-of-copyright classics from literary masters such as Shakespeare, Poe, Carroll and Conan Doyle. The texts are available as zip files or plain text documents and you can download a PC reader from *www.microsoft.com/reader/*. While you're there, download the Read in MS Reader plug-in which will let you convert the texts to MS Reader format using MS Word 2000.

Q How can I remove the predictive text facility which automatically, and annoyingly, tries to fill in the web address I am entering into the browser box?

A In Internet Explorer 5.0 and above, go to Tools – Internet Options – Advanced and uncheck both 'Use inline auto complete' boxes. By the way, if users of later versions of the IE browser type a word into the address box then press and hold the Ctrl and Enter keys simultaneously, the program will insert the www and .com automatically to save a bit of time and effort.

Q When I download a program from the internet, the transfer rate in the dialog box starts off quite high (15 to 20KB/sec) then rapidly reduces (to between 4 and 5KB/sec). Why does it slow down and does the time of day make any difference?

A The burst at the beginning of a download is caused by a buffer or cache filling with data and has nothing to do with the latter figure which is your true download speed. The time of day, however, does have an effect on performance. Internet speeds can start to slow dramatically from around noon as the US comes online. For that reason, it is probably advisable to download larger files at breakfast time in the UK while you download your toast.

Q I have been asked to design a website for my village but am unsure what type of web hosting ISP I should use. What would you recommend?

A I particularly like the hosting service at *www.lunarpages.com* which offers a massive 800MB of space for your pages and excellent technical support, all for around £60 a year. An alternative is to use a free, advert supported service such as *www.freeservers.com*. It offers 12MB and some basic DIY web creation tools. Whatever you choose to do, you will need to be familiar with the rudimentary aspects of HTML and file uploading.

Q How do I lodge a complaint regarding cybersquatters?

A Domain name squatting, or the unscrupulous use of legitimate brand names on the web, has been a thorn in the modem since the early days of the internet. Many countries are starting to recognise the owner's right to recover hijacked domain names, for example the US has passed the Anti-Cybersquatting Consumer Protection Act. The World Intellectual Property Organisation (*www.wipo.org*), a Geneva-based body, also arbitrates in domain name disputes, although it has come under fire recently for some of its more erratic decision making.

In the UK, the courts are the key and an action for trademark infringement or passing off via a website is now considered a realistic option. TMDS (*www.tmds.com*) will keep an online watch out for your brand name for an annual fee, although the first port of call is to see whether your domain registrar has an arbitration service.

Q I don't always use the same computer to access the internet, is there any way to store my favourite website bookmarks online on a web page?

A One option is to sign up for the neat volunteer run Backflip service at *www.backflip.com*, where you can store your bookmarks free of charge. Alternatively, check out the rather wonderful PowerMarks bookmark manager from *www.kaylon.com*, which has an online bookmark service included in the $24.95 price. Once you have this type of service set up, you will be able to log on to your own private area from any PC to search and access your bookmarks.

Q Are there any software packages which will let me log the time I spend online and give me an accumulated time and cost for my internet sessions?

A Intercent 2K2 from *http://intercent.finiware.nl/en/* is a free software utility that will track time and expenses online using a clever interface. The program is very comprehensive and allows you to tailor just about every aspect of your service provider and phone charges. It's not perfect, however, and you will have to input your own telephone rates for the UK.

Q Every time I try to access my Internet Explorer favourites offline, my PC tries to connect to the internet. What am I doing wrong?

A Internet Explorer's offline reading function needs to be configured properly to make the most of it. In IE 5.0 and above click on Favourites – Organise Favourites from the menu, not the icon. Select and highlight the address you want to access offline and click the 'Make available offline' box.

This will bring up a Properties button which will let you schedule how often you want updates to be collected, decide how much of the site you wish to download and even set up a system which will alert you by email when the page changes.

Q **I want to take my laptop to Spain to access the BBC and** *The Sunday Times.* **Can I dial into my UK ISP by putting 00 44 before the normal number?**

A Many 0845 ISP phone numbers are classed as non-geographic and therefore cannot be accessed from abroad by adding international codes, otherwise you could indeed do as you suggest. You may be lucky with your particular number, so check before you leave. If it's a no go, your choices are either to set up with an ISP that has a standard geographic access phone number, check to see if yours offers one, or use an international roaming service such as iPass (*www.ipass.com*).

Q **While I'm surfing a box keeps appearing on screen which says: 'Security Warning – do you want to install and run Flash 5.0?' How can I get it to stop?**

A The only way to avoid this is to stop surfing sites which use Flash animation software. The warning screen is not there to scare you but to give you an opportunity to install the

Flash plug-in (*www.macromedia.com/software/flashplayer/*) so you can see the site as the designer intended. Flash can be a pleasure or a pain depending on the quality of the site's design, but it is becoming increasingly popular across the internet. As ever, however, the choice is yours.

Q **I have some digital photos I want to share with relatives overseas. Can you recommend the best website to create albums for others to view, as many seem to be interested only in pushing the sale of photo prints.**

A My personal favourites are the Fotopic site at *www.fotopic.net* and Shutterfly at *www.shutterfly.com*. Both offer free membership, have been around for a while and provide a good range of services. I've bored more than my fair share of friends and relatives with holiday snap albums uploaded at these sites. In general, keep precautionary back-ups of all the photos (or any other files for that matter) which you upload to websites. You never know if the service will suddenly change terms drastically or disappear, as happened with me once, taking your precious memories with it.

Q I am just about to start using a cable modem internet service. Can you suggest some anti-hacking software as my system will be 'always connected' to the internet?

A One of the most popular software products for this purpose is Zone Alarm from Zone Labs (*www.zonealarm.com*). It's free for personal use and is designed to shield your PC from unauthorised probing and access. I now install it on my PCs as a matter of course.

Q I recently subscribed to a home-user ADSL internet service. Is it possible to connect up more than one computer to the USB modem that is supplied with the service?

A You can share internet connections – whether ordinary modem or broadband – either by using the internet sharing (ICS) feature of Windows or by downloading a software package such as the $30 EZProxy from *www.lavasoftware.net/en/content/ezproxy/overview.htm*. I use a hardware alternative called the Diva 2480 (*www.eicon.com*) which is an excellent ADSL modem and multi-user router in one small box. It's easy to set up and incorporates a wireless connection if you have a laptop with WiFi onboard. Chris Spry provides a great ADSL primer at *www.cspry.co.uk/computing/adsl_uk.html*.

Q I am interested in online banking but am worried about security. Many sites seem to prefer the 128bit standard. Am I at risk with only a 40bit browser?

A A thicker bank vault door is obviously stronger than a thin one and 128bit encryption is better than 40bit, but in all cases it will take a determined and expert criminal to get at your hard-earned cash. Good encryption will help prevent crooks gaining unauthorised access to things like your password and account details while you are online, but don't be misled by trendy scare stories – online banks rely on much more than just encryption technology to secure their services. No bank is invulnerable though, either on the high street or information superhighway, which is the price we pay for modern convenience.

Q How can I temporarily disable the filtering on the Content Advisor of Internet Explorer?

A All the settings relating to content are accessed via the Internet Options – Content menu under Tools. Here you can restrict explicit sites or even restrict the amount of violence or other offensive material the browser will access. You can also lock the settings with a password if required. To disable the function, you will need to enter the password if set, and adjust the sliders and allowable content settings to your new preference.

Q I subscribe to a high-speed ADSL broadband service, and while speeds are impressive, there are sites which still seem to take forever to access. Why is this?

A Broadband is a very neat technology, but it is only one link in the whole internet chain. Access speeds will vary according to how remote geographically you are from the site you are trying to access, your computer specification and, especially, the quality of the service hosting the site.

Even the general state of the internet at the time you are online will play its part, as at certain times it can get very congested out there. All you can do is grit your teeth and wait for the pages to load properly.

Q **When I upgrade to broadband shortly will I be able to receive internet radio stations to output through my stereo system?**

A Broadband is the ideal way to receive global internet radio stations and at good quality. You can find a selection at *www.radio-locator.com/*. To pipe them to your stereo system, either connect a cable from your sound card line-out socket to your stereo's aux input port, or check out something like the MP3 Anywhere set from *www.intellihome.be/english/index.html*, which will let you listen to music streamed from your PC to anywhere in your home.

Q **I would like to set up and run an online UK message board forum centred on one particular subject. I have seen these types of forums based in other countries, what do I need to do?**

A The geek method is to cook up your programming skills, throw in a branded web domain and stir for a serious amount of development hours. The altogether more sensible option is to cheat. For smaller communities, check out the free service at *www.ezboard.com/*. You can set up your own forum in about ten minutes flat and it's well designed. Also check out *http://thinkofit.com/webconf/index.htm* for some good pointers on web conferencing tools.

Q I seem to have acquired a program called Go-Hip on my computer and can't get rid of it no matter what I do. Can you help?

A Oh yes, what a friendly little soul Go-Hip is. It's supposedly a free search site plug-in, but what the company doesn't tell you is that it also makes annoying branding changes to your email program, browser start page and search settings. Worst of all, it embeds itself into the Windows registry which makes it hard to remove. After much consumer pressure the company now offers a small free program for download which removes the little blighter. Go to *www.gohip.com/remove_browser_enhancement.html* and follow the instructions.

Q Why does my PC repeatedly try to connect up to the internet after I receive an email from one of my online subscription lists?

A This is because you have received an HTML coded message which is trying to connect back to its source to update. To disable this annoying function in Outlook Express go to

Tools – Options – Connections – Change and check the 'Never dial a connection' box. This means you will have to connect manually in future but it will remove the immediate hassle.

Q Is there any software I can use to stop my internet connection being terminated part way through an unattended large file download?

A Take a look at the $29.77 Download Wonder program from Forty Software (*www.forty.com/2002_download_wonder.htm*). This lets you keep downloads alive by simulating browser actions during the process. It also has a host of neat features including a library function so you can keep track of downloads and a 'resume if interrupted' function.

Q I intend to start using the internet in the near future. If I do so, will I be able to view sites in the Chinese language without installing any extra software?

A How you view web pages is determined by your web browser. If you are using a later version of Internet Explorer, it should automatically prompt you to download the simplified Chinese character set it needs when you browse a Chinese language site for the first time. After that you should have no problem.

Q I read somewhere that there is sometimes an additional charge levied by websites via the use of a special telephone number. Is this true?

A Strictly speaking these are not websites but private networks which establish a direct connection to their services using your telephone line and modem. They were used a fair amount in the past for private clubs, some online banking and also adult services. I'm not sure how much of it continues today, but apart from AOL most public oriented services no longer use this system, relying instead on generic internet connections via a conventional ISP.

Q I travel the world on business frequently. How can I log on to local internet providers and only pay local phone charges when I am abroad?

A There is a choice of methods. AOL users can connect via any of the many local access numbers available to subscribers worldwide, although there will be a surcharge for using the service internationally. Check with *www.aol.co.uk* for details or use keyword Global. For others, the best bet is probably to use the joint iPass/i2roam service (*www.i2roam.com*). It will cost between $3 and $15 an hour, but for frequent business travellers it could still work out cheaper than hotel international phone rates. It's also worth checking out the GRICTraveller service from *www.goremote.com*. The company charges a monthly subscription of about $20 and an access fee of around 11¢ a minute.

Q Can you recommend somewhere where I can get cheap web hosting without the adverts?

A There are loads of cheap web hosting options around, but beware geeks bearing gifts! Your £5-a-month deal may signal zero support, patchy service and indicate that your site is sharing a hard disk with 1000 others including a portly pornographer from somewhere near Togoland. This may be fine if you're only storing a basic set of hobbyist pages, but for more sophisticated needs I recommend using a service with decent support and performance guarantees. Check out *www.lunarpages.com* for an example of the kind of support oriented service on offer.

Q Do you have any advice on how a children's charity in East Africa could go about raising funds using the internet?

A Nowadays the internet is a very noisy bazaar, which means it's not easy to make yourself heard above the clatter. Probably the best place to start is with the newsgroups, communities of people who meet online to talk about their particular interests. Visit *http://groups.google.com/* and do a search on 'charities' or 'philanthropy' then join a community to start asking for help. The number one information source about the subject is probably *www.fundraising.co.uk*. It features a wealth of information on all sorts of fundraising issues, online and offline, so check it out thoroughly.

Q **I bought a 56k modem but I have never received a connection speed of 56kbps, it is constantly 28.8. Why is this?**

A The line speed of modems varies according to a number of factors. These include the 'cleanness' of your telephone line (how noise free it is between you and your nearest BT exchange), the length and quality of the physical wiring in your home which carries the signal and even the quality of the modem you are using. Basically, the more noise there is on the line, the slower the modem is likely to be because of continual error correction. Ring your telephone service provider and get it to check the line (for BT call 150) and ask it to improve the 'gain' (or volume) if necessary.

Q **Is it possible to receive an internet connection to my house through my digital satellite receiver.**

A Although there are plans to provide full internet services through a standard set-top box satellite receiver, at the moment the technology required is far too expensive to implement. This means that for the foreseeable future email is likely to remain the only internet service available to consumers through set-top satellite delivery.

There are, however, several services starting up which will offer satellite internet access to small and medium-sized businesses if they are prepared to pay the price. Typical set-up costs are around £2,000 with monthly charges of £150 upwards for very high speed access using standard 60cm and 120cm dishes. You can find further information on the Astra example of this type of interactive satellite service at *www.ses-astra.com/*.

Q I understand there is a danger that others can gain access to your PC while you are online accessing the web. Can you advise?

A For a set of definitive articles on the question of online PC security – and the lowdown on some not so good defences – read Steve Gibson's excellent Shield's Up report at *https://grc.com/x/ne.dll?bh0bkyd2*. This includes his evaluation of personal firewalls, the software now being marketed to safeguard our systems. The articles can be a little technical, but if you persevere you will understand a lot more than most about the problems. Most of the real worries will come when we are all lucky enough to own fast, permanently on connections to the internet such as ADSL or cable modems. In the meantime, ensure at the very least that you have file and printer sharing disabled from within Control Panel – Networks.

Q I intend to go travelling very soon. Can you help me identify which ISPs provide a local call facility from anywhere in the world so that I can dial in cheaply from any country?

A There are two main global roaming services available in the UK, GRIC (*www.goremote.com*). and iPass (*www.ipass.com*). Remember also to check up on local phone adapter and modem compatibility. There's nothing more frustrating than discovering you can't plug your modem or laptop into the necessary hotel sockets. Teleadapt at *www.teleadapt.com* does a range of adapters, but my most indispensable tool is a dual female-to-female US RJ11 socket, which I use to hook my modem to the phone cable coming from the wall.

Q What exactly is FTP and where can I learn more about it and basic HTML?

A FTP stands for File Transfer Protocol which is the technology that allows computer files to be moved around the internet from machine to machine. Your browser supports FTP transfers automatically, as do a number of dedicated

FTP software packages. There are several excellent resources on the web which can help you get up to speed on these and other technologies. Take a look at eHow.com (*www.ehow.com*), which has a comprehensive computer and home electronics help section. Another good source of information on internet basics is the About.com site so check out their *http://netforbeginners.about.com* for an excellent resource covering everything to do with the internet and world wide web.

Q Can you suggest a way of using the internet to trace long lost friends or relations, some of whom I have not contacted for more than 20 years?

A I recently caught up with my best friend from junior school through the services of *www.friendsreunited.co.uk*. Alternatively, you could try *www.lostschoolfriends.com*. Readers also recommend *www.find-lost-friends.com*. For wider ranging searches, check out *www.192.com* and the guaranteed no find-no fee service at *www.peoplesearchers.co.uk*. In emergencies, don't forget the Missing Persons Helpline (*www.missingpersons.org* or 0500 700 700).

Q How vulnerable are you if you do not have a firewall installed on your PC, and what are the dangers to look out for?

A The security software salesmen would have us believe there are millions of black-hatted hackers out there just dying to sniff out our bank account information if we don't have a firewall, but you are probably more likely to have your credit card details purloined by a crooked waiter in a restaurant, especially if you're using an intermittent dial-up connection.

Broadband users are a little more vulnerable than conventional dial-up modem users, so it probably makes sense for them to install a product such as ZoneAlarm (*www.zonealarm.com*). It may also be wise to avoid storing crucial confidential documents and data on your hard disk just in case.

Q How does a site know when I last visited it even though I have not supplied the information? Can this method of user tracking be used for sinister purposes?

A This is done through the use of 'cookies', which are little text files each website can deposit on your PC hard disc without you knowing. They tell the site who you are and other bits of information every time you return there.

There is a constant debate about their use and abuse, centring on the amount of information these sites collate and how they intend to use it in terms of selling us things. One side of the argument is that cookies are useful because they personalise our surfing; the other view is that they are

dangerous threats to online privacy. Check out
www.cookiecentral.com/faq/ for a round up of the subject
and details of how to switch them off.

Q **What is the best image format to use to create web-friendly graphics which are not as large or clumsy as BMP or TIFF files?**

A There are a number of choices for the budding web
designer. The most popular graphic format for artwork type
images is GIF, which also offers an impressively compressed
size even when used for animated graphics. The standard for
online photographs is JPEG, which provides excellent and
scaleable compression with a minimum degradation of
quality. Most good quality graphics editing packages such as
Photoshop (*www.adobe.com*) and Paint Shop Pro
(*www.jasc.com*) will handle JPEG files with ease.

Q **Is there any way to prevent information such as cookies being stored on my computer after I have been browsing the internet?**

A If you are using Internet Explorer 5.0 go Tools – Internet
Options – Security – Internet – Custom to choose your
cookie settings. In IE version 6.0 and above go to Tools –
Internet Options – Privacy. Be aware, though, that removing
cookies can make surfing much slower, especially with sites

that require you to register, as they will continually ask you to re-register if they can't recognise you from your previous cookie information. Some sites will even refuse to work if they see you have disabled cookies.

Q **If I see an image on a web page I would like to use as wallpaper or even utilise within my own web page, how can I grab it?**

A My advice is to refrain from risking a violation of copyright by this kind of 'borrowing'. The question of copyright on the web is coming under legal and commercial scrutiny because of the rise in the number of people misappropriating the property of others. Copyright laws protect websites from unauthorised duplication or use. This includes all the components of the site, from the smallest button to animations and JPEG photographs. My advice is to stick to the numerous websites which offer thousands of free web images for download. Log on to *www.pixelperfectdigital.com* for a good example.

Q **How complicated is it to set up a web page which can accept online credit card orders from customers?**

A Nowadays most of the reputable web hosting services will help you set up an e-commerce site – or web shop –

which can accept credit card payments for goods. The key thing to remember is that somewhere along the transaction line there must be a merchant account set up with one of the approved credit card agencies. In the first instance, check out your web host or take a look at the specialist e-commerce suppliers such as *www.paypal.com* or *http://ikobo.com*. Secure Trading at *www.securetrading.com* also supplies a range of credit card services for would-be online entrepreneurs.

Q **How can I print out the www addresses in my Internet Explorer 'favourites' listing?**

A For some strange reason Microsoft has consistently refused to add a print function for the favourites folder, which can be frustrating if you need to keep hard copy lists of your most useful sites. The long way round is to use the File – Import/Export wizard within Internet Explorer to export your favourites to a bookmark.htm file, which you can then access and print out from within IE. The short way is to download the $35 shareware package Acqurl from *www.acqurl.com* and use that to print out your selections. It's not a very pretty program but it seems to work. A 30-day trial version is available on the site.

Q Is there any way to stop the horrible screeching noise when my modem connects to the internet?

A Thankfully there is. In Windows 98 go to Start – Settings – Control Panel and click on Modem. Select your modem in the box, click on Properties and set the speaker volume to off. Voila, blessed silence. If this slider is inoperable (greyed out) then you should try entering ATM0 (that's the letters ATM and the number zero) in the modem section of Control Panel. Open Control Panel, click on the Modem icon, select the modem and click Properties. Choose Connection – Advanced and in the Extra Settings box enter ATM0. Click OK to save and close.

Windows XP users should go to Control Panel – Phone & Modem Options – Modems. Click on your modem name, select Properties – Modem tab and move the speaker volume to off.

A reader suggested AOL users who suffer with loud modem screeching noises should try the following. At the Sign On screen click Setup then go to Expert Setup. Click on the Devices/Modems tab, select the modem you use and press Edit. You can set the speaker volume to high, low or off. This Edit screen can also be used to change other modem settings.

4 · Mastering Windows

The Windows operating system dominates the world of computing. From Beijing to Blackburn, personal computers in their millions are all running a version of this popular package. Not everyone finds it easy to use, however, and many people have nothing less than a love/hate relationship with their computer. Like cats, they can be totally, screamingly, frustratingly, annoying. And, of course, the Windows operating system is what we come face to face with first in these circumstances.

In fact, many Windows problems are little to do with the system itself, but are related to how it interacts with its environment. For example many crashes and freezes on your computer can be caused by faulty third party software in printers, scanners and other USB devices.

To you it looks like Windows is playing up again, but it is more likely to be sloppy programming on the part of a very distant hardware or software company. That's why, when you get a problem with your PC, it often pays to sit back and take a moment to recall what you have added, changed or removed from your system recently, as the clue to your problem will often lie there.

Top Don't Panic Windows tips

Keep updated

All computer systems crash. There's no such thing as a crash free computer system, no matter what anyone says. One way to try to avoid problems is to keep your Windows system up to date. Microsoft operates a very sophisticated update process (use Help under the Start menu) which lets you download and install updates relatively painlessly (if a little slowly over a dial up connection).

Don't fiddle

Be cautious about messing with the core Windows settings unless you're confident about what you're doing. I suspect more problems are caused by users inadvertently deleting or altering a vital component of Windows than anything else. Is it absolutely crucial that you change the Administrator's security settings like that? Why is it necessary to alter the memory settings just because a friend said it made his system speed up? The best rule of thumb is if it ain't broke, don't try to fix it.

Housekeeping helps

Windows, like every other operating system, needs to be dusted down every so often to keep it sparkly clean. There are, for example, some well established routines for defragmenting (cleaning up) the hard drive, deleting unneeded files and removing unnecessary icons which you can use as a form of preventative maintenance. Do a search for Disk Cleanup Tools in your Windows Help menu. These won't necessarily result in a massive improvement in performance, especially if your computer is getting on a bit, but it should help to slow down any degradation.

Use your mouse

Most people don't realise just how useful their mouse really is. The pointer gives you clues as to what's happening with the program you're accessing on the screen, and if you need to gather more information about a file or image you should always use the right mouse button to access the Properties menu. Properties are the settings or information which are attached to a Windows file or procedure and can be very useful for finding out more about it.

Drive carefully

One of the most important parts of the Windows environment is the driver. This small software program is the link, or interface, between a piece of hardware and the Windows operating system itself. So, for example, a video driver will interface between Windows and the video graphics cards to ensure you receive a top-notch image on your monitor. It's the same with sound drivers for sounds, printer drivers, digital camera drivers and so on. If you are having trouble getting an add-on product to work, check the manufacturer's website to ensure you download and install the latest driver, as this will often cure a host of performance and operating problems with Windows in general.

Top Don't Panic Windows questions

Q What are WMA files and where can I get them?

A Windows Media Audio is a file format for creating and storing compressed audio material, such as music tracks. It is the Microsoft competitor to MP3, which has become the worldwide standard for storing and playing music. Windows has a built-in WMA file player called Media Player, which can also create WMA files from your music CD tracks.

Q Is it possible to delete any of the icons in the task bar and, if so, how?

A Hold your cursor over the offending icon and press the right mouse button. You should then be given an option to Exit or Remove the icon.

Q Can I make wallpaper for my desktop using my own scanned photographs?

A Yes indeed. Take a look at Frank Pleitz's excellent Wallpaper Changer for Windows (*www.wallpaperchanger.de/*). It is free, works brilliantly and will cope with any standard JPEG image file. Once you've scanned your photos, save them as JPEG (or JPG) files, load them into the software and select your preferred display option. If, like me, you're too lazy to make your own, try downloading some free wallpaper photographs from *www.wallpapers.com/*.

Q **My son has managed to move the Windows 98 task bar from the bottom of the screen to the right-hand side vertical position. How do I get it back where it belongs along the bottom?**

A This is one of those silly little problems that Microsoft should really have documented better, because it's so easy to correct when you know how. Simply hover your cursor arrow over the bar and then click and hold the left mouse button down while dragging it back to its proper position. Another trick if you want to gain a little more display space, say on a portable, is to right mouse click the task bar, select Properties and check the Auto Hide box. The bar will disappear until you hover the cursor arrow over the area where it normally resides, which is usually, of course, at the bottom of the screen.

Q Is it possible to set up a password on my computer to stop any unauthorised use?

A A very effective way to do this is to download the superb free SecureIt Pro program from Quantrix at *http://go.to/quantrix*. This well designed utility allows you to lock down a Windows computer in more ways than you can possibly imagine. It does pay to be careful when using this kind of program though. I remember one embarrassing episode some years ago where I forgot a password and ended up having to reload Windows. It is also worth noting this type of program won't stop a determined and expert assault on your machine.

Q Every time I move the icons on my desktop to another position they refuse to stay in place and return when I restart the computer. It is very infuriating. Is there any way to make them stay where I put them?

A You are an unwitting Auto Arrange victim, but there is a cure. Simply right click on the desktop with your mouse, select the Arrange Icons option and de-select the Auto Arrange setting. This will release your icons to roam freely wherever you and they choose. Remember, though, that with freedom comes responsibility!

Q Is there a way to get rid of the Windows sounds that come with desktop themes when I am playing audio CDs on my PC?

A To stop your event sounds, as they are called, go to Control Panel – Sounds and under Schemes (in Windows XP you will find this under the Sounds tab), select No Sounds. This will disable the noises for as long as you need. When you want them back, simply reverse the process and re-select the scheme you want. You can also experiment here by altering some of the sounds for Windows events such as Windows Exit or New Email arriving.

Q I seem to have lost all audio functionality on my PC. Even the Windows background navigation sounds are barely audible even with the speakers up full. What has gone wrong?

A It may be that you adjusted a sound setting inside a program, game or video playback and it has stuck at that level for all your Windows settings. Take a look at your sound mixer settings. If you double click on the little grey or yellow speaker in the Windows task bar, a mixer box will pop up with volume settings for each of the audio components of your PC. Make sure they are set at a reasonable level and that no important mute boxes are checked.

Q I keep getting a Windows error message that tells me 'This program has done an illegal operation – dah dah di dah'. What is it and how can I eliminate it please?

A If I could wave a magic wand and cure this widespread problem I would now be writing this from a large yacht anchored off Turtle Island, Fiji. As it is, all I can suggest is that you try to eliminate any possible causes one by one. Faults on Windows PCs are almost always directly connected to your last major action, such as installing software or hardware. If you get a fault it probably means the software installation (or driver installation for things like printers or scanners) has done something naughty with your Windows files.

Take a look at *www.easydesksoftware.com/gpfs.htm* for a fairly comprehensive explanation of the phenomenon and suggestions of how to get round it. Warning: it may contain a bit too much technical information for some, in which case I suggest a lie down in a darkened room for a while afterwards.

Q **I have a laptop running Windows 3.1 which only has floppy discs. How can I install a browser to be able to look at my emails please?**

A The 16bit Opera browser located at *www.opera.com/* should fit the bill perfectly. If you need a dialler as well, try the Windows 3.1 resource page at *http://lightspeed.alturl.com/* where you can find an older version of MS Internet Explorer for Win 3.11 available for download onto four floppy disks. Take a look also at the OB1 browser at *www.offbyone.com/*.

Q **My Windows won't shut down properly any more, what can I do?**

A This is one of the most common problems with Windows and can occur because of any number of factors including a corrupted exit sound file, a damaged device driver or even a duff hardware component. Microsoft has acknowledged the problem on its website and has included a shutdown troubleshooter in Windows itself. Access it by clicking on

Start – Help – Troubleshooting – Shutdown and Startup
Troubleshooter. For a comprehensive set of solutions on the
subject visit *www.aumha.org/a/shutdown.htm.*

Q **I want to pass on my old computer to my grandson, but
need to clear off Windows 98 and reinstall it. Can this job be
tackled by an amateur?**

A The reinstall process is fraught with potential traps for
the unwary and should only be undertaken by those with
a strong disposition, a large pot of tea and a degree in infinite
patience. If you are still determined, there is a step-by-step
guide at *www.dansdata.com/sbs30.htm.*

Q **I cannot make the defragmentation program work on my
Windows 98 computer. Is there any alternative?**

A Defragmenting is meant to reduce wear and tear on
a hard disk, but more often than not it actually increases wear
and tear on the poor soul trying to carry it out. First, always
run the defrag program in Windows Safe Mode to prevent
other programs interfering with the process – Safe Mode can
be accessed by holding down the left shift key during the
computer start-up procedure.

Q I keep receiving a Windows pop-up notice that my 'virtual memory is too low' and is being adjusted. Is this a problem?

A This message normally appears when several programs are running simultaneously, when there is too little memory in the machine or when you are working on large files such as high-resolution digital photographs. This is generally a friendly warning, so simply shut down any unnecessary programs and carry on, but if it happens frequently, consider investing in some extra memory.

Q I often receive error messages when playing clips from sites with Windows Media Player. Can you help?

A Most media-clip problems arise from not having the right decoder software installed on your system. The ultimate solution is to upgrade to the latest player from *www.microsoft.com/windows/windowsmedia/download/default.asp* or download a free alternative such as Xenorate from *www.xenorate.com/*.

Q I understand Microsoft has withdrawn all support for Windows 98. Should I upgrade to XP?

A Microsoft has indeed stopped offering free support and upgrades on Windows 98, although there is self help and paid support still available. Find out more at *http://support.microsoft.com/default.aspx?scid=fh;en-gb;LifeWin*. Upgrading to XP is probably unnecessary, unless your current system cannot run your preferred software. I wouldn't bother if your machine still works well, especially because the computer's memory will probably need to be bolstered to make the most of XP.

Q Why, when I try to open photos on my computer, does a message appear saying 'There was a problem loading the file specified when running the accessibility wizard'?

A I suspect this is a Windows bug that may need patience to overcome. If you do not use the accessibility functions, uninstall them by going to Control Panel – Add & Remove – Windows Setup – Accessibility and unchecking the box. This problem can also occur when the file you are opening is not associated with any program. To check and correct this, highlight a photo file, right click the mouse and select Open With then select the correct program (try Internet Explorer if there is no photo-editing software). Finally, tick the box that says 'Always use this program to open files of this type'.

Q I keep getting svhost.exe errors and have to restart my computer. Why is this?

A The svhost file is a traffic cop that controls programs running on Windows XP and 2000. It sounds as if you might have been infected by the Blaster worm virus. If you're running Windows 2000, download and install the SP4 patch from Microsoft (or make sure you have Service Pack 3 installed) then apply the Blaster worm patch. More info on the problem can be obtained at *www.microsoft.com/security/incident/blast.mspx* and *securityresponse.symantec.com/avcenter/venc/data/w32. blaster.worm.html*.

Q How can I erase entries from my Recent Documents menu?

A In Windows 98 right mouse click on your task bar at the bottom of the screen, select Properties – Start Menu Programs and click on the Clear button in the Documents Menu box. In Windows XP, access the Properties – Start Menu tab as before, but then you'll need to click on Customize then the Advanced tab and Clear List.

Q I used to have a typeface called Signet Round Head on my old Windows PC but lost it when I upgraded recently. Have you any idea where I can download it again?

A I'm assuming that you mean Signet Roundhand which was supplied with certain models of the HP Deskjet printer. You can find a replacement at *www.softpaw.8m.com/stuff/fonts/Fonts.html*, but please check you continue to have the right to use the typeface before you risk infringing a copyright. To install a new font, go to Control Panel – Fonts and select File – Install New Font and browse to the location of the downloaded TTF file.

Q How do I install a screensaver from a CD ROM into the screensaver menu on my PC?

A Screensaver files are supplied as .scr files. To copy a screensaver from disk simply select the relevant .scr file (eg screen.scr) with the mouse's right button and select copy. Then Paste it into the Windows folder on your computer (in XP they go in the Windows/system32 folder). To switch it on, go to Control Panel – Display and access the Screensaver tab, where you will be able to select it. For a selection of free and commercial screensavers try *www.freesaver.com/*. If you have a good 3D video card and want to mess with the cat's leisure time, download the stunningly realistic Marine Aquarium saver from *www.fish-byte.com*.

Q My internet provider's phone number starts with 161, but Windows insists on placing a 0 in front of the number when it dials up. How can I stop this happening?

A The simplest way to do this in Windows 98 is to clear the Use Area Code and Dialling Properties box in dial-up networking. Click on My Computer then select Dial up Networking. Right click on the dial-up connection you use (it will show something like your modem or ISP name) and press Properties. Underneath Country Code uncheck the Use Area Code box. Now enter the exact phone number you want to use including the area code in the Telephone Number box and the program will use that instead of adding in area codes.

Q I seem to have disabled the standby function on my Windows 98 PC. How can I get it back please?

A Go to Start – Settings – Control Panel and click on System. Click on the Device Manager tab and then click on System Devices to expand it. Check to see if there is an Advanced Power Management Support entry showing. If so, select it and press Remove. Restart the computer and run the Add New Hardware wizard from within Control Panel, which should automatically reinstall the APM standby function. If the entry is not present, you should install it by following the instructions at *http://support.microsoft.com/support/kb/articles/Q188/1/34.ASP*.

Q The DVD drive on my PC doesn't automatically play the disc when inserted. Is this because it is not set up properly?

A Your PC should have a setting which controls the 'autoplay' function of the CD or DVD drive. The function is activated from within the Windows device manager. Go to Control Panel – System and click on Device Manager. Select the DVD drive name in the list with right mouse button and click on Properties – Settings and ensure the 'Auto insert notification' box has a tick in it. Click OK to exit.

Note also that for the function to work, the CD or DVD itself needs to have a file named Autorun.inf in its root directory. Despite the obvious design advantages of the feature, many software developers – to their shame – still do not implement this capability. On Windows XP go to Start – My Computer – select the DVD drive with the right mouse button and then the Autoplay tab where you can set up the required actions.

Q How do I stop the user name and password box appearing in Windows 98 every time I start up my PC?

A The log-in box is used by Windows 98 to set up individual user profiles, so things like favourites, desktop and dial-up passwords are configured for each user of that PC. If you are the only user or want all users to have the same settings, you

can go to the Microsoft support site on the web at
http://support.microsoft.com/support/kb/articles/Q152/1/04.asp
to find out how to remove the log-in box (basically you
change the Primary Network Logon to be Windows Logon).
But you should only do this if you are not connected to
a local area network.

Q **Is there a site from which one can download the euro symbol?**

A Most later versions of Windows and hardware products
have euro support built in. To test your version of Windows
using the UK keyboard layout, open up your word processor
(not Notepad) and press the AltGr and 4 key simultaneously
(or turn Numlock on and hold down the Alt key while
quickly typing 0128 on the numeric keypad). Macintosh
users can press Shift, Option and 2 together. You should then
see a euro character pop up on screen. If this doesn't work,
it may simply be that your machine isn't properly set up for
the symbol yet. Check out the Microsoft Euro help page at
http://support.microsoft.com/default.aspx?scid=kb;en-
us;188081 for some guidance or try downloading the euro
symbol font pack from
www.fonts.com/fontservices/services_home.asp?con=euro.

Q When downloading or installing new software there are generally instructions to turn off all other programs. Is there an easy way to make sure no programs are active?

A The simplest way to check is to press the Ctrl, Alt and Delete buttons on the keyboard simultaneously. This will bring up a small box detailing all of the programs which are running on your PC. To stop a particular program, simply select it and press the End Task button which will close it down. Leave Explorer, Systray and Rnaapp alone though. You may need to do this process more than once for a particular program entry. Alternatively, try the Enditall 2 utility from *http://home.ptd.net/~don5408/toolbox/enditall/*.

Q Every time I start my computer up, it is running in safe mode. How do I get it back to normal mode?

A Safe mode indicates there is a problem with Windows, either a hardware or software driver conflict, an incompatibility or some damage to the registry. Your PC is therefore loading with minimal drivers so you can test what the problem is. You may need to uninstall/reinstall an errant driver or hardware add-on to get it back to normal. Unless you are technically proficient, I suggest a trip to your nearest computer dealer.

Q I am running Windows 98 and have noticed a huge folder called CABS in my Windows directory. Can I delete it?

A Despite anything you might have heard, this is not some cunning Microsoft plan to corner the taxi market, but rather a way of storing the essential Windows install files on your hard disk in case you ever need to add or restore drivers to your system. You should not delete this folder unless you have a Windows 98 install CD lying around that you can insert in an emergency.

Q I often download videos from the internet but they will not play, despite the fact I use Quicktime. Why is this?

The clips may be in another format such as Windows Media or Real Media. You can overcome this by going to *www.microsoft.com/windowsmedia/* or *www.real.com/* to download and install their free players.

Q Is there a viable alternative to Windows? I'm heartily sick of Windows 98 crashing all the time.

A There are many who share your dismay, although, there are also millions who happily use Windows software day in, day out with little or no difficulty. If you are determined you could consider switching to the Apple or Linux operating environments, although in either case you will need to relearn your computer skills. Why not try Windows XP? It is a lot less prone to the dreaded crash than any of its predecessors.

Q **I recently received a 'Divide Overflow Error' message on my PC. Can you tell me what this is and how I can prevent it happening again?**

A Microsoft calls this a Divide Error and it's basically one of a multitude of arcane error messages which Windows throws up for various reasons ranging from buggy software to clashing hardware components. The company suggests sufferers start Windows in safe mode and if the problem doesn't appear this will indicate it is likely to be a software or driver problem. It then suggests loading each Windows component individually to home in on the exact cause. For more detailed information go to Microsoft's knowledge base at *http://support.microsoft.com/default.aspx?scid=kb;en-us;82710*.

Q **Is it true that when you delete a file on your computer it is not permanently removed from your hard drive and can be retrieved later by someone who knows what they're doing?**

A That is very true. The file is not deleted but simply tagged as erased and left intact on the disk. This is partly why computer crime fighters are able to retrieve supposedly deleted data and prosecute wrong doers who think they've covered their tracks. Law abiding folk who want to delete files properly need to use something like the freeware Eraser program from *www.heidi.ie/eraser/*.

Q How do you get into the Windows system to put a U in Favorites?

A Unfortunately I believe the matter is currently out of our hands on this side of the Atlantic. There were unsubstantiated reports that the European Commission was looking into the matter as part of its probe into the anti-competitive activities of Microsoft Corporation, but this is purely hearsay. Until such time as the missing U can be relocated and returned to its rightful place, I am afraid we will all have to grit our teeth and try not to let it color our judgement of American software too much.

Q I believe that by using various Alt key combinations I can insert foreign accents – such as an acute – into documents. Where can I find a list of these options?

A The quickest way to get an accented vowel is to press the Alt-Gr key (normally on the right-hand side of the space bar on a UK layout keyboard) and the relevant letter simultaneously. Alt-Gr and the E key, for example, gives you é. For other special keys in Windows go to Start – Programs – Accessories – System Tools and look for the Character Map. If it's not there you'll need to install it from your Windows CD. Another Alt key map can be found and printed off from *www.kelseypub.com/irc/charmap2.html*.

Q **I want to print some screen images off my PC for a friend but the 'print screen' key on my computer doesn't seem to work. Please help.**

A To call it a 'print screen' key is really a bit of a misnomer. When you press it what actually happens is that a 'snapshot' of your screen is recorded and placed into the 'clipboard' memory of Windows for use when you need it. To access and print the captured image, open the application you want to use, for example Word or Paintshop, then select Edit followed by Paste from the menu bar at the top of the screen. The image will then be copied into your application and can be printed at will. Remember, though, that the image will be stored in memory only as long as the computer is switched on. Turn it off and you lose it.

Q I would like to upgrade to Windows XP but fear my indispensable old DOS-based diary program will not run. Can you advise?

A You're right to be concerned, since the new version of Windows now only contains a DOS emulator, not the real McCoy. However, if your program works properly under Windows NT or 2000, and if it does not try to access the hardware directly, you may get away with it by using XPs compatibility mode. See if you can test it out on a Windows XP machine before you hand over your cash, or check with the software maker to see if it has an XP upgrade version.

Q Is it possible to retrieve files which have been erased from the Windows Recycle bin, and if so how?

A Try out Fast File Undelete from *www.dtidata.com/*. This $29 utility scans your disk for any deleted files and will let you retrieve the ones which have not been overwritten and can, therefore, still be recovered. Remember that in general, if you do accidentally delete a vital file, you must attempt recovery immediately to have a reasonable chance of success. Take a look also at the free Handy Recovery program at *www.handyrecovery.com/*.

Q My son tested a free Mickey Mouse game on our computer recently. Now somehow we have irritating pictures of the creature all over our PC when it is switched on. How can we remove them?

A You are the unwitting victim of a Windows theme attack and are lucky you didn't get the whole kit and kaboodle desktop takeover version as sometimes happens. The quick solution is to pop along to *www.desktopmaster.net/clickbank/index.htm* and download the $19.95 Desktop Manager theme management program. It will allow you to remove, change and manipulate all the aspects of your Windows theme settings, including sounds, wallpaper, icons and screensavers.

Q I would like to regain some space on my PC hard disk by deleting the 'Temporary Internet Files' which take up a lot of megabytes. But what exactly will this do to my computer and browser?

A These temporary files speed up your web browsing sessions by storing elements of websites you have previously visited on your computer so you can access them quicker when you revisit the site (instead of downloading them again). If you delete them you may, therefore, notice a slowdown in your browsing performance. If that's acceptable, try also going to Tools – Internet Options – Advanced in IE 5.0 upwards, and under Security check the 'Empty temporary files when browser is closed' box.

This will delete the files automatically after you finish each surfing session and close down the browser.

Q **I can't get the sound to work on my PC, despite trying everything I can think of to fix the problem. What am I doing wrong?**

A There are a number of procedures to run through when checking sound problems. With Windows 98, first take a look in Start – Settings – Control Panel – Sounds. Click on Default Sound (or Default Beep under the Sounds tab in Windows XP) and see whether the preview button turns black. If it does and you can't hear anything that means your sound system is working, but the noise is not getting to your speakers for some reason. Check speaker wiring and sound card connections.

If the button remains grey, your sound card is not working properly. It may be in conflict with another component or is not being recognised by the PC, so try uninstalling and re-installing the sound card drivers. If all else fails, you may have a faulty sound card which needs replacing.

Q **Is there a simple way to get a printout of the files and folders that are on my PC?**

A If you have a small number of folders, you can open Windows Explorer which will display your folder information and then press the PrtScn (print screen) button to save the screen to the clipboard. You will then be able to paste the information into Word and print it from there. It's a bit cumbersome, but it works. A nice software alternative is the free Widget Print Directory V3.1 which lets you print out files, folders or directories as you require. Check it out at *http://widgetech.com/freeware/printdir3_1.shtml*. A reader also recommended *www.karenware.com*.

Q **When I run Scandisk in Windows 98, I regularly get a message saying Scandisk has restarted ten times and that I should close some applications down, even when I don't have any programs running. Can you advise?**

A Windows can be exceptionally perverse in many ways, and one of them involves running tasks without telling anyone. For example, if you have Microsoft Office installed on your machine, it is almost certain the Find Fast utility (which indexes the files on your PC in the background to make for faster retrieval) will be running during your task. To turn it off, go to Start – Settings – Control Panel and click the Fast Find icon. Click on Pause Indexing under the Index menu.

Q **After upgrading from Windows 98 to Windows XP one of my software programs no longer works. What are my options?**

A After an operating system upgrade it's often worthwhile checking the driver download section of your computer manufacturer's website. Go to Support and/or look for Downloads or Drivers, then download and install the correct files for your PC model, component and version of Windows. When software products are involved you should also visit the program vendor's website. An alternative is to try a generic driver site such as *www.driverguide.com/*.

5 · Computer hardware

Hardware is, basically, the computer bits that are solid and can be touched, thrown around the room, kicked and otherwise abused. That's not to say you can't abuse software, but the real point of software is not the disk it comes on, but what happens when you install and run it.

Hardware is extremely complex. We may treat our PC as if it were no more than a toaster when we unpack it from its box, but in reality the technology that goes into even the cheapest models is mind-bogglingly advanced. The technical complexity of a modern PC makes Nasa's lunar module which landed on the moon back in the 60s look positively prehistoric. So let's try to have a little bit of respect for that plastic cube we sometimes treat so casually.

Don't bash it about unnecessarily and try not to throw cups of coffee over it. Don't leave a laptop out overnight in the sub-zero temperatures of your car boot then bring it into a centrally heated living room and fire it up immediately. Give it a little time to warm up and for any condensation to evaporate safely. Just try to be a little thoughtful and your computer will appreciate it. A lot.

Top Don't Panic computer hardware tips

Keep it maintained

Computers need maintenance, just as a car needs servicing.
Keep an eye on the amount of hard disk space you have left,
since a PC will slow down significantly if it does not have
enough to run a proper swap file for your memory.
Defragment the hard drive regularly, delete files and uninstall
programs you don't need, and generally try to reduce
unnecessary file and program clutter on the machine.

Watch your addition

It can be very tempting to keep adding shiny new peripheral
devices to your computer. Generally there is no problem
adding one or two. However, the more add-ons you have, the
more the potential for driver, software or hardware conflicts,
and if you are not experienced enough to spot the signs, you
may end up with a bit of a mess on the end of your power
cables. That's not to say you shouldn't do it, just be cautious
until you are more familiar with computing and know a little
more about the pitfalls.

Read the manuals

I can't stress enough how important it is to read your
manuals. Yes, some are ridiculously obtuse and, yes, most are

hideously complicated to navigate but, believe it or not, they can help solve some of the more mundane problems. In particular, pay attention to installation guides, especially for printers and USB add-ons, which often need to be installed in a particular way.

Ask another user

When it comes to computing, the internet really is your friend. Chances are that if you've experienced a problem with something, others have too. All you have to do is find them and see if they have a solution you can use. The best places to start are the user forums on the manufacturer's website. Failing that, do a Google search, especially if you can locate a conversation about your particular product, problem or error message in the Google Groups forums (*http://groups.google.com*). Perseverance is the key.

Top Don't Panic hardware questions

Q My PC has suddenly started crashing. The screen goes black then automatically reboots and the 'enter password' box is displayed. Can you suggest anything I can do?

A There are so many possible causes for the dreaded PC crash that it is almost impossible to find a cure at long distance. The problem is that the PC is a huge mix of components, all of which rely on each other. Your crash could be caused by a faulty memory chip, a duff video card driver or even an incorrectly configured modem.

A lot of problems, however, can be fixed simply by re-installing your Windows system, since more often than not a sudden onset of the PC crashes is caused by Windows developing a fault which causes it to conflict with one of the components. If the re-install fails, try gently placing a large hammer on the desk next to the keyboard while fixing the monitor with an icy stare.

Q Is there a charity that will accept old PCs and printers for use here or in poorer countries?

A Computer Aid International has set up just such a service to provide computers for schools and community organisations in developing countries. This registered charity is always on the lookout for equipment and would be delighted to hear from you. You can visit its site at *www.computer-aid.org/* or call it on 020 7281 0091. You could also contact the folk at *www.free-computers.org*, who offer recycled computer equipment free to schools and other educational establishments. But bear in mind that very old equipment may be too dated to offer any value as a charitable donation.

Q My old computer seems to have slowed down quite dramatically recently. Should I upgrade it or simply buy a new one?

A I suggest you think about putting your old friend out to pasture and buying a new one. The problem is there are quite a few crucial aspects to an upgrade: the processor, memory, hard disk and video card to name but a few. Once you add up the cost of these it's often cheaper to buy a completely new machine. Buy the best you can afford and hopefully it won't be obsolete by the time you get it out of the shop.

Q My new PC keeps freezing. What can I do?

A Computer freezes can be caused by a number of things, none of which involve arctic temperatures. It may be down to a faulty component (eg a memory chip), duff software or a clash between two add-on products, all of which can make locating the problem a tedious process of elimination.

I would suggest you take the machine back to the shop and get them to fix it, since it should still be under warranty. They could try swapping out the main components and/or memory boards to see if that makes a difference, or check if the fans are all working as, strangely enough, overheating is a common cause of crashes.

Q **Suddenly my PC has stopped recognising the CD ROM drive, although it still plays music CDs for some reason. Can you help?**

A There could be several reasons for this, varying in severity. First of all pop into your local PC dealer and buy a CD drive cleaning kit, as often such problems are simply caused by dirty internals. It could also be a loose cable, which will require a competent person to open up the case to jiggle the flat grey ribbon cable. Ultimately, of course, you may need to reinstall your drivers or consider replacing or upgrading the CD drive unit.

Q **What is the best way to maximise the life of a laptop computer's battery?**

A The people at Toshiba inform me that while it is fine to keep a laptop plugged into the mains all the time, you should occasionally unplug it to let the battery drain before charging again. You do not generally have to run down a laptop completely before recharging though. Charging and recharging does no harm to a battery, although it will eventually need replacing. Visit *www.laptop-batteries-guide.com* for further useful information.

Q I have just bought a new PC but the picture does not fit properly on the screen. Can it be fixed?

A All computer screens come with adjustable settings that determine the height, length and position of the onscreen image. It sounds as if one or more of the settings is out of whack, or the video card and monitor have not been installed and set up properly. Either return the system to the shop to have it adjusted or spend some time with the manual and look up monitor adjustment. Visit *www.animalhead.com/monitor.html* for some additional tips.

Q I recently bought a laptop in America but I am having problems running UK software. Is this a form of region coding?

A Regional coding only applies to DVD film titles. Software from any part of the world should run on a laptop from any country as long as it has the correct language and operating system support installed. Check if your machine meets the minimum specification for the software.

Do remember that buying computers from abroad can carry an element of risk, as warranty repairs and technical support are often unavailable.

Q I bought a PC game for my child, but it will not run on our computer because it needs a video card with 'hardware transform and lighting'. Can I get round this?

A You have been trapped on the upgrade escalator. Modern games are often designed to work on computers that are no more than two years old. It is sloppy and not especially fair, but that's the price of progress. Either seek a refund or visit your local computer dealer and buy a video card, such as an ATI Radeon or Nvidia model. Ask the dealer to fit it unless you know your way around a computer's internals. Remember, it always pays to check any program before you buy it to ensure the minimum hardware specification matches that of your machine.

Q I am upgrading my old PC and would like one with automatic switch-off to save energy. Is this available?

A New computers come with some fabulously sophisticated power-down options for conserving energy. To activate this feature on a Windows XP machine, go to Start – Control Panel and select the Power Options icon.

The Power Schemes tab will let you create any number of personal set ups for powering down your monitor, disks or machine automatically, as required. Check your PC manual for other power options, including 'wake on ring', which will power up a dormant PC when a call or fax arrives.

Q **What's the best thing for cleaning a laptop screen or flat LCD monitor?**

A You need to be quite careful with this, because you can leave nasty streaks, turn the plastic cloudy or ruin the coating on the screen by using water or chemical and abrasive cleaners. Even paper towels are not recommended because they can scratch. Spectacle cleaners or a 50 per cent dilution of isopropyl alcohol will work, but the easiest option is to buy the £11 Klear Screen LCD cleaning pack, which comes with special fluid and a soft cloth, from a computer shop.

Q **What is the most efficient way to back up my computer?**

A My current back-up system comprises a fast 40GB external hard drive from *www.storagedepot.co.uk* coupled with the excellent True Image 7.0 software from Acronis (*www.acronis.com*). The software is scheduled to automatically create a mirror image of my computer's hard disk once a week, with incremental updates, including recent changes, every night. The result is a safe archived image of my computer that is only about 12 hours out of date. Any problems and I simply restore and continue.

Q My very old TV needs replacing and I was wondering whether, if I get a PC, I can use the same monitor for both BBC1 and browsing?

A You certainly can watch television on a PC monitor, especially with the fabulously crisp LCD flat screens now available. But, to be honest, the hassle outweighs the benefits by a long way. Either you have to set the PC up as a television with a TV card (see *www.hauppauge.co.uk*) and have it in your living room (and they're still a bit noisy) or you will have to lug the screen back and forth and buy a separate TV tuner box to use it for both purposes. My advice is to keep the two separate if you possibly can.

Q Where can I find information and tips to help me with my computer? I find it most irritating not being able to progress any further than basic knowledge.

A The Government sponsored site at *www.learndirect.co.uk* (or on 0800 100 900) should provide some pointers to beginners' computer courses in your area and you may even qualify for a grant or discount. Alternatively, check out the rather fine nationwide home tuition service Hairnet at *www.hairnet.org*. The company provides teaching for all ages, but focuses on silver surfers over the age of 50.

Q How can I transfer some important files from my Amstrad 9512 floppy disks to my Dell Windows 95 laptop?

A Ansible Software (*www.ansible.demon.co.uk/ai/order.html*) sells a PC software conversion package called ailink for £19.50, which will let you convert 3.5-inch floppy disk data from Amstrad to PC format. Alternatively, if you only have 3-inch disks, you may need to use a mail-order service such as the one from Luxsoft (*www.luxsoft.demon.co.uk/lux/lconv.html*). It charges around £5 per disk plus VAT.

Q I've recently purchased an Apple computer. How can I can get some basic help on getting the most out of it?

A I've heard good things about The Little iMac Book by Robin Williams (no, not that one), which apparently offers some useful advice to all those setting out on the Apple computer road. It costs £13.99 from *www.amazon.co.uk*. Or you could roll up your sleeves and spend a little time at *www.ultimatemac.com/*, which bills itself as the biggest and most useful Macintosh page on the web.

Q I use a computer for significant periods each day and have heard a lot recently about health issues arising from monitor emissions. Should I be worried?

A There have been a number of health scares associated with the prolonged use of computers, especially in relation to the emission of electromagnetic radiation. Research is continuing, but so far the official line is that there is little or no evidence to suggest a health risk from exposure to the electromagnetic fields associated with the use of monitors. You should try to avoid working for long stints in front of a screen in any case, particularly to prevent eye strain and the like.

Q How can I transfer all my business pricing information, which is stored on an ancient Olivetti word processor, to my Windows PC?

A For complex tables and columns, one way would be to print them out and try a specialist document conversion service such as DocuShop (*www.docushop.co.uk* or 07786 734414). It charges around £1.20 a page to transfer printed information to a PC compatible disk, with a £25 minimum. You may also be able to convert your Olivetti disks to PC format using a disk conversion service such as AL Downloading (*www.aldownloading.co.uk/dataconv.html/*), but remember you will need to have the right kind of software to read the resulting files.

Q Where can I buy an English copy of Outlook, where contacts reside in towns and counties with postcodes rather than zip codes? And where can I buy a colour printer rather than a color one?

A Ah, you need the Anglophile button, Alf, located under Computer – Settings – Special Relationship. This little wonder will instantly convert all American computer imperialisms into wonderful Anglo-Saxon. Customize becomes customise, favorites favourites, synchronize … er … synchronize. Hint: don't spend a lot of time looking for this button though, will you?

Q I have an old computer I want to donate to someone without funds who would like to access the internet. Will it be difficult to make it internet capable?

A Depending on its age, you may find it hard to bring it up to a good enough specification to run modern internet software. However if the PC is a 386 and above, with 8MB of RAM, a mouse and hardware modem, you could try using the rather brilliant QNX 'internet on a floppy' solution. Download the free software from *http://public.planetmirror.com/pub/qnx/demodisk/modem/qnx demo.zip*, follow the instructions and it will install a full system for accessing the internet – including a dialler, colour graphical web browser and operating system – onto a standard 1.44MB floppy disk. Reboot your PC with the floppy in the drive, enter the ISP dial-up details and it will locate the modem and log in. This excellent tool will also work with laptops using PC card modems.

Q I am about to buy a new computer. Is there a way to move the files from my old machine to my new PC simply and cheaply?

A One neat method of transferring your old machine's contents to the new one is to use PC Relocator from *www.alohabob.com*. This clever package transfers all your old settings and data including applications, bookmarks, internet connections and email messages. You connect the two PCs with the cable, fire up the software on each and off it goes. Prices start at $29.95 for the version that comes with a parallel cable.

Q How do I stop my PC turning itself on whenever my phone rings? It is so irritating.

A There's nothing worse than a phone hog, so be firm and tell your computer to get its own phone line. Alternatively, go to its BIOS set-up area – typically accessed by pressing F2, Esc or the Del key on boot – and disable the 'wake on ring' feature. This is a power management feature on newer PCs for those who want to call in and connect to their PCs from distant locations.

Q **I would like to buy my daughter a computer for her coursework at school. Do you have any suggestions?**

A Bearing in mind the basic kind of work that needs to be done at school and the tough environment, you don't really need anything too expensive. A nice budget laptop from a reputable high street retailer would probably fit the bill. I believe several, including Comet, now offer models around the £500 mark. You could always approach the school IT department first to see if it has arranged any special deals with local suppliers.

Q **Our four-year-old PC needs updating. What are the pros and cons of PCs and Macs please?**

A Apple computers are generally considered easier to use and aesthetically more pleasing than the boring beige PC alternatives. They are also better at coping with add-ons – installing a printer, for instance, is easier on a Mac than a PC – and have a reputation for being superior computers for working on graphic arts and multimedia tasks.

Contrary to common belief, however, Apple computers do crash (like PCs) and their user friendliness can be a mirage when it comes to some of the more complex but necessary computing tasks. There is also a large disparity between the amount of software available for the PC and the Mac. For every Apple title there are probably 50 PC alternatives, which could be a restriction if you wanted to expand your use of the Apple later on in its life.

Q **I don't plan to remain in one place for very long and would prefer to have my own laptop computer to avoid using internet cafés. Is there a pay-as-you-use laptop computer on the market?**

A There are a number of companies which offer this sort of ongoing laptop payment service and it is really just a matter of finding a reputable one and negotiating the right deal. Some of the car hire companies are also now starting to rent personal organisers such as the Nokia Communicator alongside mobile phones, so it may be worth enquiring with the smaller, more aggressive, companies in this market. A good starting point could be to do a search for computer rental companies in your area at *www.yell.co.uk* or, in Ireland, */www.goldenpages.ie/Search.asp*.

Q **Where can I go to trade-in my laptop computer?**

A Your best bet is to take it to your local PC dealer and see if he is interested in some sort of deal. If you're having trouble locating a retailer near you, do a search for 'computer systems' on *www.yell.co.uk*. Alternatively, visit *www.ebay.co.uk* and learn a little about online auctions.

Q **I start college next year and need my own PC. Can you advise on where to look for budget models?**

A We're entering a buyer's market for PCs right now, so make the most of it. Beware of buying too cheap, however – as with everything else, you tend to get what you pay for. If support is an important issue, spend some time reading online and magazine reviews to find companies which consistently score top marks in user satisfaction polls. By the way, don't be fooled by those mail-order special offers which provide everything bar the kitchen sink along with the basic PC – they often mask some very dodgy quality PCs.

Q **I never turn my PC off, but now some friends have told me it is probably better to turn the box on only when needed to reduce wear and tear. Is this true?**

A This is a hugely contentious issue. I keep my PCs on all the time to save me the irritatingly long Windows boot up, switching them to standby whenever possible to conserve power. Others say it is better to switch off to avoid voltage spikes and preserve hard disks and other components. Either way, it probably makes little difference to the lifespan of your computer, which will be obsolete long before it wear outs. Remember, it is the monitor which is the real power hog, so keep that powered down on standby or switched off as much as possible.

Q **I am thinking of getting a laptop in preference to a desktop computer but have heard that laptop screens are bad for your eyes. Is this true?**

A Many people actually think the LCD screen on a portable computer is better for your eyes than that of a standard desktop, because it does not flicker as do all tube-based screens. Laptop screens have historically offered a lower image specification than good quality desktop monitors, but these disadvantages are growing less each year and are still considerably outweighed by the benefits. I much prefer using my Toshiba notebook computer for everyday work.

Q **With the plummeting price of hard disks is it feasible to install a second one in my PC to use as a safety back-up?**

A I definitely recommend the use of external hard disks, if only to make it easy to do back-ups of your important data. There are some great USB 2.0 and Firewire based drives on

the market, which are very fast and well priced. Take a look
at the range at *www.storagedepot.co.uk*.

Q **Is it possible for two of us to play a computer game
together by connecting my old and new PCs?**

A It really depends on the game you have. Most of the
modern games come with what's called a multi-user mode.
This means you can either play using a proper network (like
you get in an office), across the internet or directly together
(head to head) as you suggest. To do the latter you need
a 'null modem' cable, which you can find in most computer
stores, but you must establish the game's multi-player
settings properly – check the manual for details.

Q **What's the cheapest and best way of running PC programs
on my Apple Mac?**

A You will need an emulator, of which there are currently
two main makes – VirtualPC
(*www.microsoft.com/mac/products/virtualpc/virtualpc.aspx?
pid=virtualpc*) and the Blue Label Power Emulator
(*www.lismoresystems.com/*). They range in price from \$35 to
\$250 but please don't expect blistering performance or 100
per cent compatibility. Check out *www.macwindows.com* for
a good overview of the issues.

Q Every time I switch on my PC the clock shows the incorrect time and occasionally the wrong date. Is there a way of fixing this?

A Your poor PC sounds like it's suffering from a flat CMOS battery, which is what keeps time when it is switched off. They generally last five or more years and may need to be professionally replaced. Check in your manual for details. In the meantime, you could download the free webtime 2000 utility from *www.gregorybraun.com/webTime.html*, which will sync your PC clock automatically using your internet connection and a US atomic clock.

Q Every so often, when typing on my laptop, the cursor skips back or forwards a few words or lines, which is very annoying. Can you suggest why it does this?

A The erratic cursor is something that I too suffered from in the past. Then one day I looked more closely and noticed that every so often the heel of my palm brushed against the mouse pad as I was typing and sent the mouse cursor skittering across the screen on a seemingly random errand. I cured it by using a wrist rest while typing, which helps to keep the palms raised.

Q Suddenly every t that I type has a g attached to it, and every y comes with an h. Like this almosgt everhy time. What is causing this?

A Either something sticky has been spilt onto your keyboard causing these adjacent keys to depress together, or your keyboard is heading for that great desktop in the sky. You could try cleaning it with Ultraclene or PC Buds – check *www.af-net.com/products/af_catalogue.asp* for stockists. If that doesn't work, it's a trip down to the local keyboard emporium I'm afraid.

Q I am very disappointed by the sound quality of my laptop computer when used to watch television broadcasts using an add-on tuner. Is there any way round this?

A Most portable computers are simply not designed to produce great sound from their integral speakers, primarily because space and battery life are at a premium and high powered speakers consume too much of both. You can, however, augment the tinny internal speakers with a set of purpose built external ones which you can find at most good computer dealers.

Q **Why do some standard CD drives fail to recognise and read the disks I have created using my CD-RW unit?**

A First off all, ensure your PC does not have the DMA access box ticked in the CD ROM properties tab in Device Manager. Second, ensure you are using good quality blank disks rated for the speed of your particular drive and, third, always do a complete format of the new disk and not just a 'quickie' version. If the target CD drive still fails to read the disks, it could be because it is too old or out of spec to recognise the new CD-RW standard properly. To recover missing or corrupted files from errant CD-RW disks use the excellent $49.99 CD/DVD Diagnostic from Infinadyne at *www.infinadyne.com/*.

Q **My PC refuses to remember the screen resolution setting I set for more than a few sessions. Why is this?**

A Your monitor is sulking. Did you treat it badly? Sneer at it once too often? Or could it be that Windows 98 – as so often – has 'forgotten' to install the proper monitor driver for your particular screen and uses instead the generic plug-and-play setting? Go to Control Panel – Display and click on Settings – Advanced. Under the Monitor tab click Change – Next and then 'Display a list'. You can then select the make and model of monitor you are using from the list rather than relying on the generic driver. If you can't find your monitor listed, you may need to get a software driver file from the manufacturer or try *www.driverzone.com*.

Q **I am moving house shortly. What do I have to do with my PC to avoid losing any files? Can I just switch it off and unplug everything?**

A First, back up all your crucial data onto floppy disks, a USB flash memory drive (eg *www.flashusb.com/*) or any other media you have available, just to be safe. Also try not to jolt the system box too much in transit, as hard disks are very sensitive and a sharp shock could spell the end of a beautiful friendship. This also helps to avoid jogging any internal components or boards loose. Apart from that, PCs are really quite resilient.

Q **Is there any way to start up my computer with the number lock key off as I never use the pad for numbers?**

A You have a choice. The first option is to go into your PC's BIOS set up – check your manual for details, but it's usually done by pressing the Esc or Del key as the PC is starting up – and search for the setting which lets you set Numlock Off as the default. Alternatively, take a look at the free Autonumlock utility from *www.cybervertex.com/software.html* which will automatically turn the numlock key off or on depending on which software you load.

Q My father bought an expensive laptop five years ago, and although it is in perfect working order it has no CD ROM drive and only 16MB of RAM. Is there a cost-effective way to upgrade it to access the internet and use CD ROM software?

A The short answer is … maybe. You can get an external CD ROM drive for around £80 and, yes, you may be able to find extra RAM for the machine from *www.laptopshop.co.uk*. But at the end of the day, you will probably still end up with a laptop containing a sub-par video card, processor and sound capabilities for running most CD titles. My advice is to think about a trade-in or straight replacement.

Q I need to replace my PC. Should I get a laptop or a desktop model, and do you have any pointers?

A Stay away from laptops if you are a game playing type, since most will not handle high resolution game graphics well. However, for everyday computing chores such as browsing, email and documents, portables are great and well worth the price premium over desktop PCs. I use a svelte Toshiba Tecra laptop (*www.toshiba.co.uk*) as my main machine. It's silent, lightweight and its ultra compact form means I can take my whole office with me on my travels.

Q How is it that the sound from my laptop PC speakers is fine except when listening to a DVD?

A The DVD player on your portable is probably trying to deliver 5:1 surround sound to your speakers, which means you're not receiving the correct audio signal. Try changing the audio settings in the DVD software player to stereo and under Windows 98 check Control Panel – Multimedia – Audio (Windows XP: Control Panel – Sounds & Audio Devices) to ensure you have the optimum speaker set up selected. Finally, make sure your general volume levels are set correctly by double clicking on the small speaker icon in the Windows task bar at the bottom of the screen.

Q Is there an optimum amount of RAM memory to use in a computer and is there such as thing as too much?

A Rather like cheesecake, you can never have too much computer memory, although only if you run programs that need it. It is not really worth upping your memory if all you do is write the occasional letter to Points of View using your word processing package. But if you manipulate a lot of images, run multimedia programs such as video editors or play games, adding RAM will almost certainly assist performance in one way or another.

Q Since suffering dampness in the recent floods, our PC has become almost lethargic, sometimes not booting up at all. Could it have rheumatism and is there anything we can do?

A I'm afraid computers really hate the damp, so it helps to try to keep them out of wet surroundings as much as possible. If this is impossible, try putting a cover over the system box and monitor at night, or ensure that you keep the room well aired, so the moisture does not settle on its insides. Sometimes you can correct the immediate problem by placing fan heaters in the room to help dry out the worst affected components.

Q My PC regularly comes up with 'out of space' messages even though I appear to have lots of space left on my D drive. How can I get round this?

A You're suffering from an attack of what I call 'data silt', which is the naturally occurring build up of data on your C drive. One way to combat this is to uninstall all unnecessary programs (go to Control Panel – Add/Remove Programs to start the process) and also make sure you install all future programs to your D drive and not the default C drive. You do this by selecting a different drive location during the early part of the installation routine, usually by clicking on the Custom or Browse buttons and replacing the

C with a D in the location box.

To avoid this problem in the future, start installing programs onto the D disk and, if possible, move any bulky data files, such as photographs and music tracks, there too. You can also help regain lost disk space by going to Start – Programs – Accessories – System Tools to use the Disk Cleanup tool.

Q **Sometimes my mouse pointer flies off the screen and a series of menus flash across the screen randomly. How can I stop this happening?**

A First of all check if you have fluff or dirt inside the roller enclosure of your mouse. Open up the bottom by sliding off the ball cover, clean out any rubbish which has accumulated where the ball sits and refit. If this doesn't work you may have a corrupt or clashing mouse driver installation. Go to your Control Panel via the Start menu and test your mouse settings thoroughly. If everything looks normal, you may have to install new drivers from the website of your mouse manufacturer or from *www.microsoft.com* to fix the problem. If all else fails, you may need to consider retiring the poor little chap.

Q What is the expected working lifespan of a laptop computer, assuming it is reasonably well cared for?

A The two main consumable items in a laptop PC are the batteries and the LCD screen, and it is impossible to say how long these will last because of people's differing usage patterns. The back lights of most screens are rated at around 12,000 to 15,000 hours of use but can often be workshop replaced, and batteries can also be substituted once they stop holding their charge properly. A major laptop killer is accidental damage, though, so do take care when moving it around.

Q What is the difference between standby and sleep mode on a computer, and is one a better power saving feature than the other?

A Basically they are very similar, and while sleep (or hibernate) mode is probably more 'off' than standby mode, there's no significant difference in terms of power savings. The biggest power saving on a PC comes from switching off the electricity hogging monitor. I keep my computer in hibernate mode when I'm not using it, which also helps speed the boot-up time considerably. Check your manual to see if your model can take advantage of this power saving setting.

Q Is there a way to disable the endlessly infuriating and intrusive caps lock button?

A I know just what you mean. There you are thrashing away at that important document and, bam, in mid flow you inadvertently touch the caps lock and get a stream of UGLY BIG LETTERS. Apparently Fabio Falsini has also suffered at the hands of the annoying key and, being a programmer, has done something about it. Visit *www.falsinsoft.cjb.net/* and download the First Cap freeware utility. It will let you disable Numlock and Capslock as and when you want.

Q I have noticed a lot of adverts recently claiming you can record a DVD video disk on your CD-RW drive. Is this true?

A You are right to be suspicious. What these dubious ads are offering is a method of creating video CDs on your PC which, although possibly playable on many of the latest DVD players, will definitely not be DVD quality. To create proper backups of your DVD titles you will need a PC with a DVD recorder drive and some proper software.

Q I'm due to replace my ageing PC and am considering an Apple as I am tired of the glitches I seem to have with conventional PCs. What should be my main considerations?

A First, take stock of your existing software and see whether you are happy with the Apple alternatives. Although you should have no problem transferring data between versions of popular software such as Microsoft Word, other software may prove problematical. Also set aside a familiarisation period for getting up to speed with Finder and other Apple interface differences such as the single button mouse. There's a neat beginner's guide at *www.macoptions.com/os85/* with links to the latest Apple operating system.

6 · Computer peripherals

Time was when a PC was considered to be fabulously useful because it could add up a column of spreadsheet cells and give you a total at the bottom. Nowadays the little beige box has grown into a multimedia megalith, capable of doing tasks that were the stuff of science fiction 20 years ago.

Most of this new found flexibility has come about because of the rise and rise of computer peripherals, the devices which can upgrade the performance and capabilities of the PC exponentially. Inkjet printers now give us the power to run photo print laboratories in our living room and modems let us talk to the world, while video editing products and DVD recording drives give us the chance to emulate Steven Spielberg with our Tenerife holiday footage. We can even chat to friends 3,000 miles away in glorious colour video using nothing more than a £30 webcam and a simple software program.

The growth in the power of wireless technologies such as Bluetooth coupled with useful connection points like Firewire and USB mean today's PC is a veritable Swiss Army knife of a product, capable of doing just about anything the boffins can come up with.

Top Don't Panic peripherals tips

Edit your images

Inkjet printers have revolutionised home printing and
nowhere more than in the production of photographic prints.
We can now print out glorious photos in a full range of sizes
and formats, as long as we are prepared to meet the shocking
cost of the ink that's used. To help reduce the costs, print out
your first copies in draft mode, so you can tell whether the
composition and page layout works, and only then go for the
best quality. Remember also that you don't need to print
every image. Edit your images on screen and choose only the
very best before you print. This will save you the cost of
paper and ink.

Handle disks with care

CD and DVD recordable drives, also known as burners for
some strange reason, are great tools for archiving data and
storing important stuff like photos and email messages. But
there are things to watch out for. Do be careful how you treat
the CD or DVD disks. Don't expose them to too much
sunlight or humidity, and take special care of the label side.
Never write on them with a ballpoint pen, only with a special
CD-friendly felt tip. To ensure maximum future
compatibility, avoid using re-writeable (CD-RW or DVD-RW)

disks for important data, always use 'write once' CD-R or DVD-R disks instead. Finally, pay a little extra and avoid buying very cheap blank disks, as they are likely to have been manufactured to a less stringent standard and will deteriorate faster.

Install a powered hub

Once upon a time there was the serial and parallel port and that was how you connected your peripheral. Today we can connect to the PC via USB, Firewire, WiFi, Bluetooth, Uncle Tom Cobley and all, but USB is currently the most common method and will probably remain so for a few years. If you plug too many peripherals into one USB socket you will eventually exhaust its power and the devices will stop working. To overcome this, install a powered hub which you will find at your local computer dealer. Be careful also when installing USB peripherals, as many have to be plugged in at a particular time and have the drivers loaded in a certain order.

LCD or CRT?

One of the most overlooked peripherals is the monitor, which is surprising really since it is the bit we stare at all day. The big question nowadays is whether it is worth investing in a flat LCD screen instead of a bulky conventional CRT monitor. For those with space constraints, there's no question that a flat screen makes a lot of sense. However, for others, the benefits are not so clear cut. Look at the alternative technologies running side by side in a store if you can and see if you prefer the clarity and crispness of LCD or the warmth and all round visibility of CRT. One day LCD screens will probably replace CRTs completely, so enjoy the luxury of this choice while it lasts.

Top Don't Panic peripherals questions

Q I have 30 CD-R disks full of photos, but some have been corrupted even though they are stored away from light and heat. Any advice?

A Cheap blank CDs are not a totally secure investment when it comes to archiving data in the long term, so vital files should also be stored on external hard drives or removable disks whenever possible. Cheap blank disks that are transparent seem to be particularly vulnerable to corruption over time, so buy only ones with a thick coating on the label side – I use disks from Imation. Finally, use CD-friendly pens.

Q When I plug my digital camera or scanner into my computer's USB port, the system restarts itself. What can I do?

A This could be caused by a corrupt or clashing software driver for one of the devices, or the computer's USB port may be unhappy sharing space with something new. Try upgrading the drivers for the devices (look on the manufacturers' websites) or see whether installing a powered USB hub helps (one option is the Belkin USB Economy seven-port hub, £29.37 from *www.dabs.com*). A handy troubleshooter can be found at *www.usbman.com*.

Q I don't have a television so I recently purchased a PC/TV card to watch the occasional show. Do I need a TV licence to do this?

A Hear that knocking at the door? That's the TV detector folk come to explain that in their world a TV tuner is a TV tuner, whether it's housed in a posh walnut cabinet or stuck in a large lump of gorgonzola. Time for a quick visit to the Post Office, eh? Or do the deed online at *www.tv-l.co.uk*.

Q I have to trail a wire around the house to connect my computer to the telephone socket for internet access. Is there an easier way?

A I would suggest the BT On-Air Wireless Modem (£39.99 from *www.bt.com/*). This two-piece digital gadget combines a small wireless 56kbps modem that fits into the USB port of your computer with a box that you plug into your phone line socket. Install the software, input your settings and the two will connect wirelessly to let you surf the web from anywhere in the house. But be aware that the range may be severely curtailed – to six or seven metres – if there are several walls in the way.

Q I have an analogue camcorder and a Windows XP PC. How do I connect my camcorder to the PC to make my own movies?

A You will either need to invest in a video graphics card which includes a video input socket, such the ATI All-in-Wonder (*www.ati.com/uk/*), or purchase a dedicated video editing system. The Pinnacle Studio MovieBox DV product, for instance, comes with an external attachment box which will accept video input from a wide range of devices including televisions, VCRs and digital and analogue camcorders. The package, including editing software, costs £299 and you can find more information at *www.pinnaclesys.co.uk*.

Q Are unbranded inkjet printer cartridges worthwhile? They are so much cheaper than the branded ones.

A There are many types of printer ink cartridges to choose from, as well as the 'fill your own' ink suppliers. If you are not that fussy about quality, these should be fine; otherwise, it is probably worth forking out the extra money for branded supplies. Many of the cheap inks do not have the droplet characteristics that will produce the best results from modern high resolution printers, and refills can cause printer nozzles to block up and fail. You may also notice that cheaper inks fade much earlier than branded long-life inks.

Q While in Italy recently I tried to connect my modem to a telephone line but it did not seem to recognise the different dialling tone. Is there any way round this?

A Open up the Control Panel in Windows and click on Modems. Select your modem (in Windows XP select the

Modems tab first) then Properties and under Connections uncheck the box saying 'Wait for dial tone before dialling'. (In XP you will need to select the Modem tab then Dial Control.) This will let your modem become dial tone agnostic and happily connect up anywhere from Cheam to Outer Mongolia.

Q **My granddaughter loves the computer but she cannot manage the mouse. Is there any way to have child-sized mouse and a normal one connected at the same time?**

A This can be done by connecting the two mice to the machine with a Belkin USB Economy four-port hub (£20 from *www.dabs.com/*) or a USB-to-PS2 adaptor cable (£18 from *http://mcsx.co.uk/shop/hardware.htm*). By the way, the KidzMouse range (*www.rm.com*) features delightful squeezy mice without any awkward buttons.

Q **What is the difference between CD players that play MP3s and those that handle only standard disks?**

A MP3 audio tracks are compressed in a special way, so an MP3-friendly CD or DVD player is required to play them. MP3 tracks can be converted to the ordinary audio format on a computer with software such as Burrrn (free from *www.burrrn.net/*).

Q Is it possible to watch normal terrestrial television stations such as the BBC and ITV channels using your PC?

A Yes indeed. You will, however, need to buy and install a television module with integral tuner to do so. The most popular models are internal plug-in cards which start at around £25, although an interesting alternative is the £40 WinTV-USB from Hauppauge (*www.hauppauge.co.uk*). This is an external device with a 125-channel cable-ready TV tuner which plugs into your PC's USB port to give full-screen TV on your monitor.

Q My teenager blocks the phone line for hours while on the internet. Is there any device that will tell me when someone is trying to phone me?

A Ah, the joys of sharing life with a teenager – the affection, the thoughtfulness, the moody sulkiness if thwarted. The Internet Alert Manager (*www.otherlandtoys.co.uk/product404/product_info.html*) is a £38.95 box which hooks up between the phone socket and your computer modem and lets you know when someone is calling while you're surfing. It works by listening to the call waiting tone, so you will need to pay for this service from your telephone provider.

Q **Is there any way I can connect my old parallel-port zip drive to a USB-only laptop?**

A Quite a few people are becoming stuck in obsolete connection traps of this kind now that USB is the standard way to plug add-ons into your computer. In this case, you need to be creative, as a conventional USB to parallel-port converter will not work. Try the Elan SP230 PC Card adaptor (around £211.50 from *www.peak-uk.com*) which should work fine with your old Iomega drive. Of course, it might make more sense to bite the bullet and buy a Zip 250 USB drive (£56.99 from *www.amazon.co.uk*).

Q **How can I improve my machine to make a multimedia disk run smoothly?**

A Running other programs while accessing the disk can lead to a drop-off in multimedia performance as your computer tries to juggle multiple tasks. Check if you have any unnecessary programs running in Windows XP by pressing the Ctrl, Alt and Delete keys together. Click on the Applications tab of the Windows Task Manager box that comes up and make sure there are not too many programs running. To shut down a program, click on it and press the End Task button at the bottom of the box. But be careful that you do not shut down something important or you will crash or freeze your machine.

Q I have a wireless internet (WiFi) card in my computer and would like to connect to my dial-up internet account without wires. How can I do this?

A I have not yet managed to find a WiFi modem but there are a few Bluetooth models around. The Socket Cordless 56K modem is a battery powered dial-up modem that will connect wirelessly to any Bluetooth-enabled device, including computers and PDA handhelds. Just plug the device into your phone line and you will be able to enjoy dial-up access from up to 100 metres away. You will need to buy a Bluetooth adapter if your computer is not Bluetooth enabled. The modem costs £99 from *www.peak-uk.com/*.

Q Where can I find a record deck to hook up to my computer so that I can record my collection of 78s to CD?

A There are a number of specialist turntables that will play vintage vinyl, but you should take extra care to avoid damaging the records with inappropriate types of stylus. Note also that 78s do not always play strictly at 78rpm, so a variable speed turntable is required. I recommend a visit to *www.videointerchange.com/vintage_78s.htm* for some sound advice on the subject. Another option is to avoid the problem altogether by using the services offered at *www.pristineaudio.co.uk/index.html*. This company will convert 78s to disk for £5 per side.

Q What is the easiest way to share a single printer/scanner between two computers?

A Take one small, nondescript beige box, add three USB ports and a dial, and you get a two-way USB printer switch. Affix a price tag of £9.99, an online shop address – say, *www.consumeit.co.uk/default.php?cPath=91_167* – and you have a handy little product to solve your dilemma.

Q Why are modem speeds stuck on 56kbps, while processor speeds, memory and hard disk sizes continually increase?

A Dial-up modem technology has reached a performance plateau, which is why we are moving to a brave new broadband world with connections such as ADSL and cable. These technologies also use modems but can handle much faster data throughput. Dial-up connections will eventually follow the dinosaurs as broadband pricing comes down – for example, PlusNet (*www.plus.net*) offers always-on broadband for £14.99 a month, which is not much more than flat-rate dial-up fees.

Q I have bought a Sony digital camcorder and now find I cannot connect it to my computer, which does not have a Firewire socket. Is there any way round this?

A Fear not, help is at hand. Take a trip to *http://uk.insight.com/* and search for Instant DVD + DV from ADS. This £187.99 video capture and editing product comes with a box that attaches to a high-speed USB2 port – the oblong-shaped socket that should be found on most computers bought within the past 12 to 18 months – and incorporates a Firewire socket that will connect to your camcorder. Alternatively, you could purchase a PCI Firewire card (from £21) but installation is more complex and involves opening the computer so is probably best done by a professional.

Q Can you explain what the different DVD recording formats are?

A DVD+ and DVD- are the main standards; an R means that a disk can be recorded onto only once, RW means it can be recorded onto many times. So a DVD-RW disk is one that can be read and recorded on DVD machines many times over. Both the + and – formats will play back on the latest home DVD video players.

Q Can you recommend an external CD recorder for my laptop, as my floppy drive is useless for saving photos and artwork?

A Alas, the poor old outdated floppy. The Pikaone Ripcase external CD-RW drive looks exceptional value at £50 from *www.amazon.co.uk* – especially as it also doubles as an audio CD player. Alternatively, consider a USB flash drive, which is great for transferring small files. You can pick up 256MB models for about £60 if you hunt around. Try *www.expansys.com* or *www.usb-flashdrive.co.uk*.

Q What is the best way to transfer music from cassette onto CD?

A Connect a cable from the 'aux out' of your stereo cassette system to the 'line in' of your PC sound card, then download the £5 RipVinyl program from *www.wieser-software.com/ripvinyl*. Follow the instructions and you should be a happy camper. Alternatively, consider installing a Plus Deck internal cassette deck for the PC (from *www.forgevalley.com*). This £128 add-on fits neatly into a CD ROM slot in your computer and will convert music from cassettes into MP3 or WAV files.

Q Can you recommend an MP3 player that I can use to record and listen to science programmes when I go walking?

A The world is certainly not short of portable audio players, from small versions that plug directly into a computer's USB port to capacious hard disk models that can hold every album track ever recorded with room spare. For portability, consider the WeWa WMP6803FM from *www.mp3players.co.uk*. It is reasonably priced at £79 and has a great set of features, including an internal FM radio you can use to record programmes directly into the player.

Q I have just bought a new PC but cannot connect my Midi piano keyboard to it because there is no joystick port. What can I do?

A Hear sweet music by investing in a USB Uno plug-in Midi adapter from *www.procass.co.uk/MIDI_Interfaces2164.htm*. It is a little pricey at £38, but the maker has a good reputation and it comes with an integral USB cable and Midi connectors as standard.

Q I have been diagnosed with motor neurone disease, which affects my ability to speak. Can you help me locate a suitable communication device?

A A good place to start is probably the Communication Matters site at *www.communicationmatters.org.uk/* where you will find lots of useful information on all aspects of specialist communication needs. Take a look also at The Grid text-to-speech software (*www.sensorysoftware.com/software/pocketgrid/index.html*), which works on most Windows mobile devices.

Q Why are audio CD-R disks much more expensive than the data variety? I've never encountered any problems using cheaper data ones for making music CDs. Is this just a way of extracting more money from the naïve public?

A The bottom line is that there is no real difference, but if you have a CD recorder deck, as opposed to a computer based CD-RW drive you will probably need to use this type of audio disk which was created specifically for the consumer market. These music-only audio disks incorporate a form of copy protection and the price includes an anti-piracy royalty which apparently goes to the music industry, hence the higher price.

Q Are there any affordable machines which will let me scan and transfer microfiche material into my computer system?

A I remember the days when microfiche was the height of James Bond sophistication, all tiny celluloid images hidden under postage stamps. Now it seems people can't wait to get shot of the stuff and move on. Ah well. Check out the EyeCom ImageMouse which is a £1,250 system specifically designed for scanning microfiche into computers.

Q I have inherited my father's 16mm home movies dating from between 1944 and 1960 and am considering having them professionally transferred to video. Should I now be looking to transfer to CD ROM or DVD?

A Transferring to DVD rather than videotape currently makes sense for every reason except cost. With the state of modern technology you can now store upwards of two hours of video footage on a single durable DVD disk depending on the quality of the picture and the compression used. Visit *www.videotodvd.info/* or *www.smarttape.co.uk* for examples of pricing and service.

Q Has there been any research to show the approximate life of printouts from inexpensive photo-quality colour printers? And what about text documents?

A Because of the relatively recent nature of the technology, it is hard to find authoritative data on the lifespan of inkjet printouts, but it is generally accepted that in many cases they may not last as long as conventional photographs. There are three components to inkjet colour print longevity – paper, environment and, perhaps most important, ink. Some printer ink colours, for instance, fade faster than others, especially when exposed to the UV rays in strong sunlight, and factors such as humidity play a part.

The manufacturers are working hard to perfect non-fade inks and long-life paper, but for now be aware that your prints may start fading within a year or so if displayed in a brightly sunlit environment. If you're worried, store them in a drawer as you would a snapshot album. If you need a print life of longer than five to seven years for text documents, look for ink and paper products bearing the term 'archival quality' or consider using UV resistant glass to protect wall hanging printouts

Q I am trying to use a microphone headset to make calls using my PC and the internet, but the system doesn't work well and keeps telling me I am using half-duplex mode. What does this mean?

A This has to do with your sound card. If you have a very old computer or sound card, you will only have half-duplex mode available to you – as opposed to full duplex. This means the equipment can only handle data in one direction at a time, so you can either talk or listen but not both together (rather like a walkie talkie set). The tell-tale sign is that you need to press the mic button or a key on the keyboard to talk and release it to listen. I'm afraid the only solution is to upgrade your sound card to a full duplex model. Note that the same thing applies to certain older brands of voice modem.

Q Is it possible to obtain a Region 1 DVD player software package so I can play these disks on my PC rather than the UK's Region 2?

A The simple answer is yes, but you will need to purchase the $39.95 DVD Region Free program from *www.dvdidle.com*. The movie industry now stands almost alone in its attempts to enforce the rather silly regionalisation of DVD content. PC DVD drives were the first products to offer region-free playback, after region unlocking software appeared on the internet for free download. Nowadays most of the Far East manufactured DVD video players will play DVDs from every region once a simple code is entered into the remote control (normally by pressing something like 0123, then the close drive or play button).

Q **Is it possible to buy a scanner, printer and computer which will print to the quality of a fine art print without spending a fortune?**

A The quality of standard PC printing has improved dramatically over past few years. Most of the 'budget' label inkjet printers from Epson, Lexmark and Hewlett Packard will now print out at astonishingly good quality resolution, in some cases with results that are indistinguishable from photographic prints. Visit a reputable computer dealer and try out several printers in your price range – you may find one with the kind of quality you need.

Q **How well do laptops play DVD films in comparison to dedicated portable DVD players, and is there any software that will enhance DVD film playback on a laptop?**

A The latest high power portable PCs have more than enough processor oomph to play DVDs and they sport large LCD screens which offer superb resolution. The best way to improve the quality of laptop DVD playback is to test different software players and see which suits. For the past few years I have been using PowerDVD from *www.gocyberlink.com* which is robust and has good features.

Q I love flight simulator games and want to buy a new PC dedicated to that purpose. Can I run both my old and new PCs on the same monitor using a selector switch?

A Don the anorak and flying helmet and pop over to *www.kvmswitchdirect.co.uk/* to check out its selection of multi PC/monitor KVM switches which will let you control multiple PCs from a single keyboard, mouse and monitor. They range in price from around £10 to more than £100, although I suggest you stay away from the very cheap products if you want to maintain performance and image quality.

Q I keep hearing about 3D accelerator cards for my PC. What are they for?

A 3D accelerators are souped up graphics cards which replace the standard video display card inside the PC and give you enhanced, high speed graphics. They provide the kind of performance boost essential for modern PC games. If you have a yen to sit in front of a screen for hours enjoying all sorts of gaming adventures or driving exotic Italian cars using your keyboard and mouse, these add-ons are a necessity. The two biggest brand names are ATI and Nvidia.

Q I have a games joystick with an old-style 15 pin connection, which is not supported by my new PC with its USB sockets. Is there any way around this?

A You need a special USB converter box rather than just a plug adapter, because USB ports incorporate electronics to identify the type of peripheral being plugged in. The Rockfire USB-Nest Joystick Converter, which sells for around £18, is available from most good computer stores or online from Reveal at
www.revealcable.co.uk/Large/1600/aa_1611/aa_1611.htm.

Q With all the latest hardware and software, is there any reasonably easy way to edit home video cassettes?

A There are some really excellent home video editing packages. If you're not too fussy about capture speeds or top quality resolution, look into one of the new external video capture and editing systems which plug into the PC USB port, saving you the hassle of opening up your machine to install a card. For example, the Pinnacle Studio MovieBox USB product (*www.pinnaclesys.com*) costs less than £150 and has received some favourable reports.

Q I am having trouble connecting devices via the infra-red port on my laptop. Do you have any suggestions?

A I have also had similar problems with my laptop recently. The major issue seems to be that manufacturers implement infra-red technology in different ways, which means many devices simply refuse to talk to each other or drop the connection every few seconds. I am afraid we will be stuck with this situation until the standard settles down. By the way, even the new Bluetooth wireless technology is experiencing problems of this kind, so we may have to wait a while before these devices are reliable.

Q Please can you tell me if I am going mad! I am sure I read recently about a small handheld device which lets you insert a memory card and view your images on a small slide show screen.

A You're not nuts. The product you mean is the Digi-Frame which accepts either flash memory cards or material on CD ROM. You can get both portable and desktop versions, which will store and playback photo slide shows of digital photographs on a small LCD screen and without a computer. For more info go to *www.digi-frame.com*.

Q I have found some really old monochrome negatives which I cannot get printed. Is it possible to do this using my PC scanner?

A If you have a scanner which has a transparency adapter option – and many do – you should be able to scan and print to your heart's content. Failing that, check out the Primefilm 3650 Pro film and slide scanner which my spies tell me offers great resolution and costs just £299.90 from *www.jessops.com*.

Q I am trying to output DVD movies from my computer to the TV screen, but so far I can get audio but no picture, what am I doing wrong?

A If you can hear but not see the DVD, you may need to look at the 'video out' settings in the Display section within Control Panel in Windows. Each video card has its own way of handling external output, so check to make sure the TV 'video out' setting is enabled properly under one of the options.

Q My 81-year-old father has recently bought a scanner to go with his computer. Are there any good guides to help him use it?

A The best scanning guide I have come across is Wayne Fulton's Scan Tips site at *www.scantips.com/*. This offers a huge amount of information on getting the best out of a scanner, from how to set it up to sending images by email. The site is free to use and there's also a book based on it which costs $23.95 plus P&P. A great example of an enthusiast site which is genuinely useful.

Q **I am looking to buy a 17-inch LCD monitor, but with so many on the market, I do not know how to choose. Can you help?**

A As you might expect, cheap is not always best, as there are a number of hidden issues associated with LCD screens, such as pixel refresh rates and connection technologies, to watch out for. If you've got the time, visit a computer store to take a look for yourself before you invest your hard-earned cash. Also check out an informative article at ArsTechnica (*http://arstechnica.com/guide/flatpanel/flatpanels-1.html*).

Q **I have been saving important images to a CD but suddenly my PC is refusing to read the saved data. Can it be recovered?**

A The disk may have become scratched or dirty, or your CD drive could have developed a problem. Try cleaning the disk with a damp or optical lens cloth in case that helps, and try it in another drive to see if the problem goes away. If you get no joy, Peter van Hove's free utility ISOBuster (*www.smart-projects.net/*) may let you read the disk and recover the files. Failing that try CD/DVD Diagnostic (*www.infinadyne.com/*), which costs $49.99 for the downloadable version.

Q I have recently installed a CD writer and wonder what difference, if any, there is between 'burning' and 'drag and drop'.

A Burning a CD is the act of actually recording the information onto the disk, while drag and drop refers to the process of selecting the files or information you want to record. To burn a CD, you drag and drop selected music files into the relevant area of your program and then press the onscreen Record button to start the recording procedure. Drag and drop is often used in other ways too, for example to simplify computing tasks such as printing or to move shopping from the car to the kitchen table.

Q Is there an easy way to create a short presentation on a CD recordable disk which will automatically run when the disk is inserted in a computer drive?

A Lots of CD creation programs take advantage of the auto-run feature in Windows, but you will need to decide on the material you will be using before making a choice. If it is solely images, consider the free Photoplayer Plus and Power See from *www.unidreamtech.com*. If, however, you want to distribute PowerPoint presentations you might try Sonia

Coleman's Autorun CD Project Creator (*www.aladat.com*), which for $50 should cope with most needs. Remember, though, that the huge variation in PC configurations out in the big world can play havoc with automatic players of any sort.

Q I have a DVD drive in my PC which will currently only play US DVD disks, but I would like also to play UK DVD disks. Is there something I can do?

A You may be able to solve your region problem by visiting *http://forum.rpc1.org/portal.php*, which contains a selection of files to upgrade DVD drives and allow you to unlock and revert the region settings. But note that these tools are only for experienced users and should be used with a great deal of caution. As the notice on the site says, you can permanently disable your drive if you are not careful. A safer solution is to use the $39.95 DVD Region Free program from *www.dvdidle.com/dvd-region-free.htm*.

Q Do you have any recommendations for a scanner that is compatible with my laptop?

A As long as your laptop has a USB port it should be perfectly at home with the latest generation of scanners. Most of the major printer manufactures such as Canon, Epson and Hewlett Packard offer a range at different prices. You will need to spend a bit more if you want to scan, say, high quality photographs at speed, though. And don't be fooled by extravagant marketing claims about resolution. Scanning at resolutions above 2400dpi is rarely necessary or practical for everyday use, since you end up with huge files which can be difficult to edit and manipulate.

Q **Is there such a thing as a video recorder for the radio? I would like to record a range of programs on various channels at different times when I'm not around.**

A Take a look at the new €210 Radio YourWay product. This innovative device will let you automatically record favourite shows. You can set it up to record daily or weekly programs. It features an internal speaker and comes with earphones for private listening. The only constraint is that it works with flash memory, so it does not have any expansion capability, which means you're limited to a set amount of recording space before you have to delete or archive the material to your computer. For more info go to *www.uhu.ch/seten.htm?/english/mp3.htm*.

Q I am trying to buy a computer for 13-year-old who is paralysed down his right side. Are there any specialist resources we can use?

A A good place to start is the charity ACE (*www.ace-centre.org.uk/*). Its site contains a wealth of information on accessibility products and issues, including lists of specialist computer equipment suppliers. Another useful site is *www.keytools.com/* which offers a full range of specialist IT products. Finally, check out Computers for the Disabled, a small charity which provides a nationwide service supplying second-hand computer equipment for those with special needs. It can be contacted on 01268 284834 or at *www.cftd.co.uk/*, and PC donations are welcome.

Q **Is it possible to add a Firewire connection to my computer and if so how?**

A You can buy add-in Firewire cards, which let you hook up camcorders or other high speed devices to your PC, from most good computer retailers. Prices start at about £60. Note that you will have to open up your PC to install these cards and get your hands dirty connecting up an internal power cable. Go to *www.adaptec-uk.com/* for an example of the type of products I mean.

Q **I have an old 1993 PC running Windows 3.1 and no CD-ROM drive. Do you know if there are still laser (or other) printers available for such a penny farthing of a machine?**

A Most of the better modern printers will work perfectly well with Windows 3.1 as long as you obtain and install the right drivers. Your problem is that you have no CD ROM which means you will either have to download the driver from the internet (try *www.driverzone.com/*) or obtain a copy on floppy disk somehow. Try your local printer dealer.

Q Lightning strikes nearby have destroyed my modem on a couple of occasions. Is there a device I can buy to protect it in future?

A That's one for the scrapbook – lightning really does strike twice. What you need is a surge protector and one which includes telephone line protection. Belkin offers the SurgeMaster at between £10 and £30 depending on specification. Some models include a warranty to cover equipment which fails while connected to its products. You'll find them at your nearest compute store or at *www.belkin.co.uk*.

Q I am touring Europe soon and would like to stay in touch with friends and family by email and perhaps digicam. Can you suggest the best set up?

A Why not look into a handheld PDA or smartphone? You will have to contact your service provider to set up your email before you travel. Most PDAs will now accept camera add-ons if they don't have them integrated, and most smartphones – such as the Sony-Ericsson P900 or Nokia 6600 – are similarly equipped.

You will have to put up with sluggish transmission speeds, even with patchy services, and you won't get the top quality images of dedicated cameras, but this is more than offset by the convenience factor. You can even buy a GPS satellite navigation module to so you don't get lost in the wilds of Belgium. Visit *www.expansys.com* for a good selection of PDAs and add-ons and *www.pdastreet.com* for an overview of the market in general.

Q **Is there any way I can use my digital video camcorder as a webcam so I can stay in touch with relatives in Australia?**

A To accomplish this neat trick you will need to buy a video capture device (aka a video grabber) to connect your PC and camera. One example is the AverTV USB box from *www.averm.co.uk/avermedia/index.htm*. You will also need a software program such as EyeBall Chat from *www.eyeballchat.com*.

Q **I have apparently inadvertently played a US Region 1 DVD more than the permitted number of times on my PC and can no longer play UK Region 2 disks. Can I reset the system?**

A You have locked the region setting by switching between playing UK and US disks more than four times, which means you are stuck with the last region you played when the counter ran out. What a ridiculous and unfair system this region coding is. If you have an older DVD drive installed, you might get round it by installing a different software player, otherwise I'm afraid you will probably need to buy a new DVD drive. Visit *http://faq.inmatrix.com/* or *www.visualdomain.net/* for an overview of the problem.

Q **I have just bought a scanner but when I scan a text document, it comes out with a lot of mistakes. Am I doing something wrong?**

A Just about every OCR (optical character recognition) software package I've come across suffers from one form of scanning glitch or another. Most get confused and output a poor result if the text is in an unusual font, patchily printed or copied, or the page is too complex because, for example, it has a lot of boxes. It's often a matter of trial and error to see which settings in your program work best. Choosing a higher scanning resolution may help, but at the end of the day much will depend on the quality of the software. Wayne Fulton's site at *www.scantips.com* is a great for scanning matters, by the way.

Q **Is there any way of printing a single frame from a DVD movie playing on my PC?**

A It is not possible to do a conventional screen grab using the 'print screen' button on your keyboard during DVD playback. The best way to capture a freeze frame is to use a software player such as PowerDVD, which comes with a neat screen grab button on its controller toolbar. You can download a limited 30-day trial version free from *www.gocyberlink.com*.

Q How can I connect my desktop PC with DVD player to my stereo system and TV?

A There are two parts to this project, the audio and the picture. To connect the audio, you will need to take a cable from the 'line out' of the sound card on your PC to the 'line in' or aux socket on your stereo amplifier. To output the picture, you will need a graphic display card in your PC with a TV-out socket to connect to your TV's Scart socket. Without this you will need to buy a special video-out box such as the £75 Ultimate XP from Stavekirk (*www.stavekirk.co.uk*).

Q I have just bought a relatively decent 3.3 megapixel digital camera and would like some advice on a printer to go with it.

A Most of the newer inkjet printers will print really decent colour photos onto plain paper, but the cheaper the printer the slower it will be. You'll have time to make a leisurely cuppa while waiting for a full colour page to emerge from most printers costing less than £100, while their faster and more expensive brethren will pump one out in less than a minute.

Epson, Canon and Hewlett Packard all have a good range, and I've been very happy with the speed and quality of my own Lexmark X5150.

Q **I would like to display the photographs taken with my digital camera on a television. Can you tell me how to do this?**

A Some of the latest higher priced cameras now have a direct digital or 'video out' port which allows you to connect your camera to the TV and show off your photographic genius. If you aren't lucky enough to own one of these, you will have to either save your photos to your PC then connect the 'video out' of your graphics card to the television, or buy one of the new generation of TV photo display devices such as the ePhoto from *www.stavekirk.co.uk/multimedia/ multimedia-detail.asp?productID=96.*

Q **Is there any way of speeding up my CD rewriter's burning speed? It is currently at 4x and I would like to upgrade it to 6x or 8x.**

A I'm afraid what you buy is what you get in this case. It's all hard coded in the design, with the speed governed by the mechanics and chipset used. You can add more memory to your computer if you want to ensure your burner runs at its optimum rated speed, as RAM is used to buffer the data as it writes. Other than that, there's nothing else for it but to schlep down to your local computer store for a shiny new upgrade.

Q I have just bought a multifunction printer/scanner/fax machine and now my PC keeps crashing. Is there any way to fix this?

A This is almost certainly a driver problem. The unfortunate thing about these fancy multi-function devices is that they are very complex, both to build and to write drivers for. Hewlett Packard, for instance, spent a long time trying to get its G45 drivers out for Windows 2000 and even then they arrived with a few glitches. The best bet is either to search for the latest drivers on the manufacturer's website or try uninstalling and re-installing yours to see if that improves things. If you have problems finding the driver you need, try *www.windrivers.com*.

Q I have a digital camcorder and have just bought a new computer with Windows ME. Can I connect the Firewire DV lead on the camera to the USB point on the computer and get the PC to recognise the camcorder?

A USB and Firewire technologies – unfriendly brutes that they are – will not talk to each other so you will need to install some sort of Firewire card inside the PC system box.

You can find a selection at *www.belkin.co.uk* or in most good computer stores. If you are prepared to step down in video resolution, you could investigate the Dazzle range of USB video capture products which will allow you to hook up your camcorder using an S-video cable and your PCs USB port. You'll find more info at *www.dazzle.com*.

Q Is there a convenient way to store images from my digital camera while I am on holiday and away from my PC?

A Consider investing in one of the new handheld hard disk storage devices, such as the Archos Gmini 220 from *www.mp3players.co.uk/site* which is priced at around £259. The Nixvue Vista from *www.portablegadgets.com/Productsindex.htmis* costs £349 but has an integral colour screen, which is great for reviewing your shots at the end of the day in the hotel room.

Q I am thinking of buying a portable MP3 jukebox player. What should I look out for before buying?

A There's not a huge amount to choose between the various jukebox players, most of which differ only in the capacity of their hard disk storage. There are several brands around and I won't single out any particular one, but I would suggest you also take a look at the smaller models which use flash memory instead of a hard disk. These 1.5 to 2GB devices typically store a thousand or so tracks rather than tens of thousands, but their extended battery time and smaller size more than make up for the smaller capacity. See the Rio Nitrus at *www.mp3players.co.uk/site/uk/rio_nitrus.html*.

Q **I use voice recognition software as I am disabled, but I keep having to unplug my PC speakers to use the headset. Is there another way?**

A I suggest you pay a quick visit to your nearest Maplin Electronics store and ask for a two into one stereo socket. This will allow you to plug your headset and the PC speakers into the one soundcard socket on your computer. It shouldn't cost more than a couple of pounds, but do make sure you select the correct size of plug adapter. I use the dual 3.5mm stereo jack version, which I believe is now the PC standard. You can also buy online at *www.maplin.co.uk* (search for 'two into one').

Q **I am about to buy a pocket PC to access email on the move using my mobile phone. Will I be able to keep my AOL account?**

A You will be fine as long as you are happy accessing your AOL messages using its web service. Connect to the internet using your new PDA and then use Internet Explorer to log on at *www.aol.co.uk/mail/aolmail/* from where you will be able to read your messages. There is also an AOL Mobile software program which you can download onto a PDA for direct access.

Q I am interested in purchasing a digital camera but can't find one suitable for left-handed users. Can you help?

A This is not a new problem – ordinary SLR camera users have been facing the same issue for years. I'm afraid that apart from the usual suggestion of holding the camera upside down to ease shutter button access, there seems to be little around to help. You can try Anything Left Handed (*www.anythingleft-handed.co.uk/* or 0207 437 3910) but I don't hold out much hope. It seems to be a righties' world I'm afraid.

Q I like to listen to music while I work on my computer but am getting tired of the poor sound quality of my integrated system. Can you suggest any reasonably priced sound card alternatives?

A The market for add-on sound cards has all but disappeared nowadays. This is less a reflection of the high quality of the factory installed sound in PCs and more to do with the fact that PC audio tends to be a pretty low priority on our shopping lists. If you really want to improve yours, look at one of the new external sound card devices such as

the Sound Blaster Audigy 2 NX
(*http://uk.europe.creative.com/products/product.asp?*) which
offers 7.1 surround sound and remote control for a shade
under £100.

Q **Is there such a thing as a voice recorder that will record minutes of meetings and subsequently convert the speech to text on a PC?**

A If you intend to have only one person dictating the
minutes, check out the Dragon Naturally Speaking 7 voice
recognition software (*www.lhsl.com/naturallyspeaking/*). This
will let you dictate into any compatible voice recorder or
pocket PC and uses voice recognition software to transcribe
the audio into text when you next connect to your computer.
Note that you will need a good specification PC and to spend
time training it for your voice.

Q **I am about to buy a digital camcorder, what PC system and specification would be ideal for video editing?**

A Invest in the best PC you can afford. Decent video
editing needs a large amount of processing power, so don't
waste time with anything under 800MHz, 20GB of hard disk
and 256MB of RAM memory. The excellent movie editing
systems for home users sold by Ulead (*www.ulead.com/*)

and Pinnacle (*www.pinnaclesys.com*) have top-notch tools
and all the hardware and software you need to satisfy that
Scorsese craving.

Q Will these new USB peripherals work with the Windows 95
operating system I use?

A I'm afraid USB and Windows 95 are uneasy bedfellows.
The later versions of Windows 95 are supposed to be USB
compatible, but my suggestion, and Microsoft's
recommendation, is to upgrade to Windows XP if you really
want to be sure of making it all work together. In some cases,
however, even an upgrade won't overcome inherent hardware
problems such as badly implemented USB technology on older
machines. The Microsoft take on it is at
www.microsoft.com/whdc/archive/usbwin98.mspx and a general
and very useful USB Q&A can be found at *www.usb.org/faq/*.

Q I recently bought two documentary films on DVD but my
computer refused to play them. Do I need to buy a separate DVD
software player or just download a DVD driver for Windows?

A To play DVD movies on your PC you do need a software
player (as well as a powerful enough processor in your PC,
of course). The market leader is a package called PowerDVD
from Cyberlink (*www.gocyberlink.com*). Version 5.0 can be

downloaded for $39.95 direct from the website. Check first though to see whether your PC came with a complimentary copy of a DVD program on a CD ROM, as many do nowadays.

Q **What is the best PC graphics card on the market in terms of performance and price?**

A Graphic boards control the image output from the PC to your screen. Top of the line cards give faster response and higher quality image resolution, especially in games and multimedia titles. The graphics card market changes faster than a rock star's girlfriends, which makes it difficult to pick an outright winner. However, at the moment, ATI and Nvidia run neck and neck for performance, with very little between them in terms of speed and price.

7 · Software applications

My dictionary defines software as 'a computer program, which provides the instructions which enable the computer hardware to work'. Without software, whether in the form of an application such as Microsoft Word, or an operating system like Windows, computers would be no more than very expensive paperweights.

The creation and maintenance of software is no easy matter – the simplest program can run to thousands of lines of tightly structured code. From the user's point of view, however, software should be invisible. It should do its job efficiently, simply and without fuss. In an ideal world, it should also learn from us and adapt to our way of working, rather than the other way round. Nowadays most commercial PC software is well priced, well written and adequately documented, although some of the larger programs such as Adobe Photoshop are so complex you almost need a university degree to operate them.

For most of us, problems occur when the programs crash, don't do what we want or simply won't install. All sufferers should remember the number one rule of software: get the latest version. Software is in a constant state of development, and the only way to be sure that it works properly with all the newest hardware components is to obtain the latest tested version. This means you may have to visit the program developer's website regularly to keep up to date, but believe me it is worth it.

Top Don't Panic software tips

Don't be a virus victim

One of the most infamous forms of software currently is the computer virus. These nasty little things 'infect' unprotected computers and can cause all sorts of mayhem, ranging from displaying silly messages to deleting all your precious data. To avoid becoming a virus victim, locate a good anti-virus package (I recommend AVG from *www.grisoft.com*), install it promptly and keep it updated using its automated service. As long as you do this, you should avoid the majority of problems with viruses.

Don't let it bug you

Despite what you may read, there is no such thing as a bug-free piece of software. Every program has bugs in it, and the measure of the product's quality is usually how well it handles and corrects these in-built faults. Most of the better quality programs rarely fail or crash, but you will definitely suffer a bug or two in your chosen software over the lifetime of your machine. In most cases the results will be relatively benign, if annoying. A frozen screen, missing menus or incorrect loading are not life threatening.

A good safety rule is to save your work often, so you escape disaster if a program goes wrong. I have my word

processor program set to auto save every three minutes.
It pays. Also ensure that you manually create incremental
numbered backups of work in progress (for example
work1.doc, work2.doc etc) using the Save As command.
That way, if you mistakenly overwrite your work file with
a blank, for instance, you have something to revert to.

Take the download road

An increasing number of programs are sold and distributed
via the internet rather than through shops. They can be
anything from simple utilities to sophisticated graphics
packages, with prices ranging from free to extortionate.
I heartily recommend exploring the world of downloadable
online software programs, both free and fee-based – there is
a veritable treasure trove of material waiting for your
attention. A good place to start is *www.snapfiles.com*.

Explore the alternatives

While we're on the subject of online programs, remember
you are not limited to using the software supplied with your
computer. Microsoft may have sewn up the operating system
market, but you do have a choice if you care to look around
for alternative applications.

For a great free web browser and email client visit
www.mozilla.org/products/firefox/. For a free office suite
which mimics the best Microsoft Office has to offer take

a look at Open Office at *www.openoffice.org/* and artistic wizards can locate a nice free graphic and image editing package at *www.hotfreeware.com/2020/2020.htm*. The truly adventurous can even replace Windows with something like the Xandros Linux operating system (*www.xandros.com*).

Top Don't Panic software questions

Q **What are zip files and how do you use them?**

A Zipping a file (or stuffing it, if you are a Mac user) compresses it to make it smaller. This makes for faster internet downloads and makes it easier to send files to someone via email. To zip a file in Windows you will need a package such as Winzip (*www.winzip.com*). Apple Mac users need Stuffit (*www.stuffit.com/*). Once you have installed the software, you select the file or files to compress from within Windows Explorer or My Computer and press the right mouse button. Select the option Add to Zip and follow the instructions. You can also zip Word documents before storing them to floppy disk for safekeeping. Windows XP now has built-in compression software, which you use by clicking with the right mouse button on any file you want to access.

Q **Can you recommend a reliable and simple program to write and record recipes?**

A For a comprehensive and feature-rich dish, take a look at the Living Cookbook (*www.livingcookbook.com*). The £19 package helps to plan meals, check nutritional details, import recipes from the web and create grocery lists. It also comes with 750 recipes. For simpler fare, try the free Recipe Manager program, which you can find at *www.nutritionanalyser.com/recipe_manager/recipe_manager.htm*.

Q **I have an idea for a computer game but do not have the programming skills to write it. Are there any companies I could approach to produce it for me?**

A I suspect that, sadly, you will receive a less than enthusiastic response from the industry. Games can cost millions of pounds to produce, and companies are reluctant to devote time and energy to testing an idea from someone outside the business. The veteran producer Tom Sloper has an excellent games-developer primer at *www.sloperama.com/advice.html*, which explains the problem.

Q **Is there any software that teaches digital photography?**

A Try Vincent Bockaert's impressive interactive e-book, The 123 of Digital Imaging (*www.123di.com*). This is available as a download for £24.50, or on CD at £30.50, and comes with 5,000 graphics and 50,000 links to help you grasp and master the intricacies of digital photography. Because it is an electronic book, interactive buttons give instant onscreen results as you try out techniques. A free demo version is available on the site.

Q In my retirement I have taken to making jams and chutneys. Is there any software available for making labels for the jars?

A One solution is to use a word processing application such as Word, or even Wordpad which comes free with Windows, to set up and store a label template which you can use repeatedly. The layout will be a case of trial and error, especially if you want to insert pretty pictures of apples and blackberries, but it is feasible if you make good use of the tab settings. Another way out of your sticky predicament is to purchase the £12 Visual Labels program (*www.rkssoftware.com/visuallabels/overview.html*).

Q Can you recommend a good address book program that prints out in a clear format?

A Try the free Personal Address Book program at *http://5star.freeserve.com/Business/AddressBooks/personal-address-download.html*. It is simple and stores conventional contact information, email and web addresses. It also has autodial and a sophisticated search feature and will print out customised layouts and envelopes.

Q Can you recommend software for creating video CDs that can be played on a standard home DVD player?

A Most of the better video editing software packages, such as Pinnacle's Studio 9.0 (£38.99 from *www.amazon.co.uk*). will create video CDs. Simply assemble your footage, edit and press the Create button to record to disk. Alternatively, consider Super DVD Creator (£18 from *www.alldj.com/sdvdc/index.htm*), which is simple to use. The video CDs should play on all but the earliest DVD players.

Q I have a family movie in MPEG format that will not play in Windows. Are there any free video players available?

A It sounds as if your opus familias may have been corrupted in transmission, so try downloading it again. Windows Media Player should play such files perfectly, although check you have the latest version (*www.microsoft.com/windows/windowsmedia/default.aspx*). For an alternative go to *www.vetch.magot.pl* and download Piotr Zagawa's excellent free Xvid;-) player. You have to admire his product naming skills, don't you?

Q I am transferring my vinyl collection onto CD, but my software copies album sides over in one chunk. Is there any way to split the file into tracks?

A Most transfer software should create spaces between tracks and even insert custom-length spaces on command. Check your documentation to see if the option exists in your program. If it does, set it to create a new track after three or four seconds of silence. If not, visit *www.rz.uni-frankfurt.de/~pesch/* and download the neat free MP3 DirectCut program.

Q Can I display photos recorded onto CDs on our television and DVD player in the living room?

A Nigel Cross's DVD PixPlay program (£12 from *www.xequte.com*) will turn your television into a super electronic photo album. Once you've used it to assemble your favourite pictures in the order of your choice, along with music and titles, you can record the result onto a video CD that will run on most DVD players. The program is simple to use, with clear instructions and help screens. A free trial is available on the site.

Q Is there a way to access all my instant messaging programs from one program?

A Compulsive chatters should head to *www.trillian.cc* and download the fab Trillian. This free program lets you chat with friends on MSN Messenger, IRC, Yahoo! Messenger and AOL's AIM program, all from the same interface.

Q Is there any software that will produce a year planner?

A Simply Calendars from Skerryvore Software (£16 at *www.skerryvoresoftware.com/SimplyCalenders*) is an all-round calendar program that will create standard month and year planners. Jan Verhoeven's Year 3 program (download from the Utilities section of *http://jansfreeware.com*) is a worthwhile free alternative but is designed only for screens and not for printouts.

Q Is there any software that will create booklets with columns and different layouts?

A Several printer manufacturers, such as Lexmark, supply printer driver software which has the option to print booklets when you select File – Print – Preferences. This is ideal for small, simple runs. For anything more ambitious, try ClickBook (*www.bluesquirrel.com/clickbook*). This is rather pricey at £30 but offers more than 130 formats for your money.

Q Is it possible to convert a PowerPoint presentation into a video CD that will run on a regular DVD player?

A Visit *http://freeware.brothersoft.com/multimedia_graphics/ screen_capture/camstudio_download_39* and download the free Windows CamStudio program. This will record your

PowerPoint presentation into a standard video file. It records all on-screen activity on the computer, so run the slideshow as normal after pressing the record button. Programs such as Nero 6.0 (*www.nero.com*) or Pinnacle 8 (*www.pinnaclesys.com*) transfer the file into video CD format and record it to disk. Press pause on your DVD player to stop the video between slides.

Q My mother is finding it more difficult to read detail on screen. Can any software help?

A Later versions of Windows incorporate a screen magnifier for reading small text, which can be found by selecting Start – Programs – Accessories – Accessibility. This may need to be installed first, so consult your manual or visit *www.microsoft.com/enable/training/default.aspx* for help. The Magnifiers website (*www.magnifiers.org/links/Cool*) also has a good selection of free and commercial screen magnifiers for download.

Q Is there any software that will let me record digital radio programmes from the net?

A The £16 SuperMP3Recorder Windows program from *www.supermp3recorder.com/index.htm* is simple to use and you can add fades or silence. A free demo with limited functions is available for download. For a sophisticated approach with superb scheduling options, however, you really need the power of Replay Radio (*www.replay-radio.com*). It is a little more complex to learn but has a great array of recording, scheduling and storage features. Apple Mac users should visit *www.rogueamoeba.com/audiohijack* and download the superb £8.70 Audio Hijack product.

Q **Is there a software package that can convert my digital photos into something more interesting, such as a drawing or a painting?**

A Pop along to *www.vpainter.com* and download the splendid Virtual Painter V4. It comes as a stand-alone package or a plug-in version that operates within image editing programs such as Photoshop or Paint Shop Pro. The program does an amazing job of converting photographs into authentic looking paintings and drawings, without you having to spend ages fiddling with settings. Prices start at £30 and a free demo version is available.

Q **I have received a mailshot offering me internet phone software and free calls to anywhere in the world. Is this genuine?**

A Free often comes with a price. While there are free worldwide computer-to-computer services that use your broadband or dial-up connection, most offers are for chargeable computer-to-telephone services at rates that are not much better than the discounted home phone services. My advice is to buy and install a PC microphone then download the free Firefly software from *www.virbiage.com/firefly/*. This will give you free PC-to-PC calls anywhere, provided the other party also has the program installed.

Q **I am looking for software that will enable me to open several web pages in a single window. Can you suggest any candidates?**

A One slightly oblique solution is to download the free Quotes-Station program from *www.quotes-station.com*. This lets you view up to 30 browser windows although, practically speaking, there is a limit to the number you can view on one monitor. Alternatively, look at the free QuadraSite browser from *www.quadrasite.com/*, which lets you open four pages at once on the screen.

Q **I have been unable to contact Symantec support to update my virus protection program and continually receive only an automated response. Can you help?**

A Technical support nowadays can be pretty patchy, whether the company is large or small. In your case, the solution is simple: find another product, such as AVG (*www.grisoft.com*) or be prepared to jump through the tech support hoops required by your supplier. In this instance, try calling Symantec on 020 7616 5600.

Q I would like to locate a Microsoft Word viewer for the Macintosh computer, but am having no luck. Can you help?

A Go to *www.panergy-software.com/products/icword/index.html/* and download icword. This shareware package lets you open, view, print, decompress and use Word files – without having Word installed on your Mac – and will handle just about all Word file formats. The software also comes with a couple of bonus features. It won't run macros, thereby protecting you from nasty Word viruses, however it will open zip and sit compressed files, which is a nice touch. The product is available on a 30-day downloadable trial after which it costs $19.95.

Q I have written 13 songs for guitar and accompanying vocals and now want to create my own CD with them. What would be the cheapest way of doing this using my PC?

A This is a great time to be a budding music star. No more hanging around draughty studios or begging favours from CD replicating people. The process is simple. Record guitar and vocal tracks to your hard disk using a cable running from a small mixer to your PC sound card. Mix and perfect tracks on the PC using a studio program. Steinberg's £399 Studio System 4 comes with a small mixer and studio software in one box (*www.steinberg.net*). Record the results to a CD-RW drive using software such as Nero (*www.nero.com*). Check out *www.homerecording.com/* for some great beginners' tips.

Q **Are programs which convert MP3 files into audio files which can be played on normal stereo systems legal?**

A Yes. Storing and using MP3 music files does not mean that you are automatically a pirate and brigand, no matter what the press and record companies would have you believe. There are plenty of perfectly legitimate MP3 music files available on the internet which can be enjoyed legally and for free. Take a trip to *www.enorgis.com/pmwiki/pmwiki.php* and sample any of the one million tracks of free music covering material from down home blues to Indian sitar. If you want to convert your MP3 files to audio check out the free Burrrn program from *www.burrrn.net*.

Q UK retail software seems to cost a lot more than the same products in the US. Are there any differences and restrictions on buying direct from the US?

A Ask a software company executive about the price difference and they'll shuffle their feet, avoid your eye and mutter something inaudible about packaging and translation costs from English into English. The fact is that most software is identical, although bigger companies such as Microsoft do incorporate local tweaks as necessary.

The proof is that the majority of software purchased and downloaded from the internet rather than a shop usually runs faultlessly in any country. The key issue for most people however is support, so it pays to make sure that whatever you buy will be supported internationally. And don't forget that if you import packaged software you will be subject to UK customs and VAT as appropriate.

Q I would love to learn how to create computer games but don't know where to start. Can you help?

A Games are serious business as you'll discover if you take a look at the wealth of resources available to budding developers. A good place to start is *www.devmaster.net*. This is a relatively advanced resource, though, so complete novices might be better trying out the DarkBasic game making program from *www.fasttrak.co.uk/* to see if they have what it takes to make that blockbuster title.

Q **Is there a good software program which can help me keep track of my growing collection of music CDs?**

A Take a look at the Windows program Music Collector at *www.collectorz.com/*. Install it and then insert your CDs one at a time into your CD drive for a few seconds. The software will scan each disk and automatically download and catalogue the content information from the free CDDB service on the internet – hey presto, no typing needed. It also has a host of neat features which makes the $25 registration fee worthwhile for those with large collections. A free trial is available from the site and there are MP3 and movie versions.

Q **We're about to buy a house that will need to be gutted and virtually rebuilt. Could you recommend any floor plan software which is easy to use?**

A Ah the joys of DIY: the dust, the smell, the crumbly rubble. Did I mention dust? Anyway check out HomePlan Pro from *www.homeplanpro.com/* which is very simple to learn. There's a free 30-day evaluation version available for download after which it costs $39 to register. Alternatively

visit *www.blackmtnsoft.com/* and see if you like the $69 Fast
Plans 7 better.

Q **How can I make an international telephone call using the
internet and my PC?**

A You will need a multimedia PC with microphone, sound
card and speakers and a piece of software which will let you
communicate via your internet connection. There are several
methods of making an internet 'call'. The simplest is PC to
PC, and this can be accomplished using a range of software
including Skype (*www.skype.net*).

If you want to phone someone on their home telephone,
however, you will need a special software package and
gateway service such as Net2Phone
(*http://web.net2phone.com/home_inten.asp*). Download and
install the software, hand over your payment details and you
will be ready to make your first call using the PC dialling
and speech software. The quality of the calls will vary
depending on your internet connection, and nowadays
internet PC to phone calls to popular destinations aren't that
much cheaper than low-cost calling card alternatives, so it
pays to check first.

Q When using Word 2000 I notice the language specification always jumps back to US English. Is there any way to keep it at UK English?

A For some strange reason the language function in Windows 98 is buried under the Keyboard settings. Go to Start – Settings – Control Panel – Keyboard and under language set your default to English British. In Windows XP you go to Control Panel – Regional and Language Options – Languages – Details. The National Anthem will start playing, a small Union Jack will ascend from the task bar and a bulldog will start barking merrily in the background. You will also thenceforth receive pukka UK English inside Word as a default.

Q Do you know of any templates or software for creating impressive looking newsletters?

A For complex newsletters with lots of graphics you will probably need a desktop publishing package such as InDesign CS (*www.adobe.com*), but for simpler versions a little imagination and a copy of Microsoft Word should be fine. Content, layout and readability are far more important components of your newsletter than the software you use. Buy a book like Newsletters from the Desktop by Grossman, Doty and Parker for some tips on design

(*http://desktoppublishing.com/bookstore/dtp-books3.html*)
and visit *http://search.officeupdate.microsoft.com/
TemplateGallery/ct89.asp* for a selection of free Word
newsletter templates to get you started (do a search for
'newsletter').

Q **Microsoft Backup will not allow me to back up my PC system
to a CD writer. Is there any other software I can use for this?**

A Test drive Simply Safe Backup from
www.simplysafebackup.com/. This combines a number of
really useful features wrapped up in a well though out and
logical user interface. As well as letting you archive your
data to CD or a remote hard disk, it will let you store your
back-ups on a remote computer using the internet and FTP.
There are several versions, ranging from a basic free program
to an all-singing all-dancing corporate edition.

Q **How can I password protect files on my PC so that only
certain people can access them?**

A Magic Folders from PC-Magic makes any folders you
choose (and all the files within them) invisible to people
using your PC. Once rendered invisible, the folders or files
can't be deleted, viewed, modified or run, which means they
can't be accidentally opened by children when you're not

around. Enter your password and they re-appear. The software costs $30 and a free trial version can be downloaded from *www.pc-magic.com*. There is also a version which will encrypt files and folders before rendering them invisible.

Q **My anti-virus software has captured several viruses on my machine. Should I leave the files in quarantine or delete them?**

A Quarantine is normally only useful when a file is infected and the anti-virus program cannot disinfect it properly for some reason. Nowadays, this is quite a rare occurrence, so it makes sense to delete these files or even switch off the quarantine function altogether, which would

avoid having infected files sitting on your hard disk. If an infected and quarantined file contains important data, send it to a specialist data-recovery service such as MJM Data Recovery (*www.mjm.co.uk*).

Q **Is there a freeware program I can use to produce my own clip-art and use it in Word 97?**

A Take a look at 20/20 from byLight Technologies of the US. As well as including most of the standard drawing and design tools such as fill, crop and bezier, it sports a few extras that make it stand out. These include Twain support for scanning, a sophisticated screen capture tool and a selection of filters and effects which wouldn't look out of place in a £300 package. The interface is not as elegant as it could be, but it works. Find out more at *www.hotfreeware.com*.

Q **Is there any software which will safely store all the PINs, passwords and user names that I seem to be collecting at an ever increasing rate?**

A There is an old saying that goes 'man with too many passwords needs to get outdoors more', which I find just a tad insensitive. I store my 155 passwords and user name details in a small Windows software package called Whisper 32. It's free – a nice gesture on the part of the author – works well and encrypts the information so prying eyes can't get at it. It will even construct passwords for the creatively challenged. Download it from *www.ivory.org*.

Q **Is there any way I can transfer word processor files from my ancient Apple LC to be read by Windows 98 on a PC?**

A The simplest way to do this is to buy a software package which will translate between these two very different computers. One of the most popular is Conversions Plus Version 6.0 from DataViz of the US. This translator can move and convert all sorts of files between PC and Mac, including spreadsheet and word-processor documents. It will also let your PC read the Apple LC floppy disks so you can physically transfer the data from machine to machine. You can either buy and download a copy of the software direct from *www.dataviz.com* or from Technomatic (*www.technomatic.co.uk/* or 08705 168 671). Have £60 or so handy when you do.

Q **I have a load of old Lotus format files on floppy disks. Can I read them with my Word program or is there a download I can get to do so?**

A Microsoft Word comes with a set of file filters which will let you access all sorts of file types from Lotus to Corel

Draw. You may need to install them from the program CD, however. To check which filters you have installed in Word go to File – Save As then click on the Save As type box and scroll through the list. To get an idea of the add-ons you can get free from Microsoft, including some nice templates for calendars and general office documents, go to *http://office.microsoft.com/downloads/*.

Q **I have dozens of programs still listed in Control Panel add/remove even though I have deleted them from my PC. Is there any way to remove these redundant items?**

A Try Nir Sofer's MyUninstaller program from *www.nirsoft.net/utils/myuninst.html* which will let you take complete control of all aspects of the installation and removal of programs in your Control Panel list. It's small, easy to use, does what it says on the box – and free.

Q **How do I convert my MP3 files so I can save them to a music CD and play them through my home system?**

A The simplest way is to download Burrrn from *www.burrrn.net*, install and follow the instructions. The software is free and will let you burn audio CDs for use with your normal CD players in the house or car. Be careful though, because there are problems with cheaper CD-R disks which some players won't read, so experiment with different brands of disk media if necessary. Do not use CD-RW disks.

Q I have an enormous project to do involving calligraphy. Is there a software package which could help?

A Handiwork supplies the $34.99 Autograph package which may suit your needs, although I suspect that to get the most out of it you will need to invest in a rather more expensive pen and tablet input system from someone like Wacom (*www.wacom.com*). In any event, you can download a trial version from *http://members.aol.com/toolbag/autograf.htm*. An alternative is ByHand from *www.sagittal.com/*, which also provides a fun way to send 'hand written' emails via the web at *www.greetingsbyhand.com/*.

Q As a swimming trainer I would like to create figures in various positions and insert them into documents as illustrations. Can you help?

A Lots of patience and money? Then visit *www.curiouslabs.com* to check out Poser 4.0. This is the definitive human figure drawing and animation package, and you can create just about anything you need with it if you have time. At £205 it may need some justification, however, so for a cheaper alternative visit *http://swimming.about.com/cs/swimminggraphics/* for a selection of swimming clip-art sources.

Q I would like to send and receive faxes from my PC. What do I need and at what cost?

A Pop over to *www.symantec.com/winfax/* and look at the WinFax Pro software. It costs around £60 and comes with just about every known fax feature you could ever want including fax to email, integration with Outlook Express address books and even a signature function. There's precious little competition in the fax software market nowadays since dear old email took over, but luckily WinFax was a good product a long time ago and has remained so.

Q I am creating acid music on my computer which is stored in the WMA file format. How can I convert it so I can copy and listen to it on a normal CD?

A You need to download the dbpowerAMP music converter from *www.dbpoweramp.com/dmc.htm*. This free Windows software will convert files between all the most popular audio formats. While you're visiting, download the equally impressive dbpowerAMP player to organise and play back your PC music collection, and enjoy the cool fully working Space Invaders game under the credits menu.

Q I often start to download a file from a site and then need to go out. Is there a way to tell the computer to turn itself off after a set time?

A You need the free Windows Shutdown software from Paul Veitch. It's a one-job wonder which will shut off your PC after it finishes your file download. However, you must have a PC with the right power management facilities and a download box which will close automatically when it finishes. It is available at *www.veitch.co.uk/shutdown*.

Q I have an ever growing number of fonts on my PC. Is there any software that can give me a printout or screen shot of them all together?

A Take a look at the free Font Glancer utility from Kyris Software at *www.kt2k.com*. It provides a quick and easy way to view all your fonts and will display the full character map in each one if required.

Q I would like to locate a bridge program which will also teach me how to improve my game.

A Check out Bridge Baron, the self-proclaimed 'Rolls-Royce' of bridge software (*www.greatgameproducts.com*). This $60 PC or Mac program lets you play and practice at seven levels so it should be suitable for all comers. For a comprehensive list of products relating to bridge, including a range of interesting handheld playing devices, visit *http://thehouseofcards.com/bridge.html*.

Q **People often send me pictures by email in a file format my computer can't read. How can I convert them to other Windows formats?**

A Save the file to your hard disk then use Jean Piquemal's rather swish Konverter from *www.konvertor.net/indexe.html* (there is an English language button). This €19.95 shareware package lets you convert to and from more than 815 audio, video and graphic file formats. It also comes with filters to enhance your images before or after conversion. The program has a couple of rough edges, including the lack of a decent manual, but is an excellent tool nonetheless.

Q **A few weeks ago I downloaded something called a Bonzi Buddy, which seemed to change all my settings. How can I get rid of it?**

A First close down the program by right clicking on the little purple monkey's body and choosing Goodbye. Then right click on the dollar sign next to your clock in the task bar at the bottom of the screen and choose Exit. Then go to

Start – Programs – Bonzi Buddy – Uninstall. Do this twice – for the bargain tool and the main program. Restart your computer and you should be done. Regrettably purple is not necessarily the sign of a real friend.

Q **Is there a computer voice recognition system that really works?**

A If computer voice recognition was a car it would be a rusty Triumph Herald. Despite the best efforts of Mr Gates and a horde of Star Trek script writers, PC voice recognition is still in the dark ages. True, we can get 90 per cent recognition accuracy, but only after laboriously training the program, speaking ultra carefully and with the mouth rigidly pointed towards the microphone. And 90 per cent still means time spent patiently editing the text. I once asked Intel founder Gordon Moore how far away he thought we were from conversational type PC speech recognition and he said at least 15 years.

Q **I want to buy a software package for garden design and cannot find a supplier. Could you recommend both a supplier and a system?**

A There are a number of domestic garden design packages, none of which are really top notch. Most offer only rudimentary graphical representations of the plants or are very complicated to use. Perhaps the best is Punch Master Landscape from Fasttrak Publishing at *www.fasttrak.co.uk*. It costs around £19.99 and includes a plant encyclopaedia, problem solver and other goodies. Don't expect a stunning facsimile of Wisley Gardens though, will you?

Q **I often download software drivers larger than 1.44MB to floppy disks and receive a message that the file is too big for the disk. How can I get round this?**

A Try using a file splitting utility which breaks it down into floppy disk-sized chunks and reassembles it again when needed. Most of the better file compression packages such as Winzip offer a similar process called disk spanning, but they can be quite complex to use. For a simpler alternative, check out Peter Crossley's free Splitter program at *http://mysite.freeserve.com/freeware01/download.htm*.

Q **How can I customise my desktop (and other) icons without using the built-in Windows 'themes'?**

A There are a number of third-party tools which let you turn your Windows environment into just about anything you want. For some really cool options visit *www.skinz.org*. You'll need a skinning package such as WindowBlinds (*www.stardock.com*) and a reasonable sense of taste, but other than that have fun. These themes can consume a lot of PC resources, though, so I can't guarantee how they'll work on yours or, indeed, what they will do to its performance over time.

Q I need to lock the keyboard on my PC as my little girl presses all the buttons when I leave it for a few moments.

A If you've found chocolate fingerprints on the delete key after hours slaving over an important project, you have my sympathies. You have three options. You can set up your screensaver with a password and activate it when you leave the PC. Or you can pop along to *http://tk.ms11.net/* and download the freeware Toddler Keys utility which lets you lock your keyboard, disable the power switch and generally make it toddler friendly (Windows XP only). Or you could just buy a new See Spot Run video and keep it close at hand for diversionary emergencies.

Q I am running a virus checker and have still been infected by a virus. How is this possible?

A Most virus checkers are only as effective as the last update of their signature files. These contain the 'footprint' or identifying aspects of the world's known viruses and need to be updated every time a new strain is found. If you have an old program of this type and have not updated it with a new signature file recently, visit the vendor's website and do so – it's worth it. Those who have no virus checker should visit *www.grisoft.com/* and download the free AVG program.

Q **Is there any software which will allow my international associates to translate letters received in English to Japanese, Korean and Arabic?**

A Pop along to the Altavista Babel Fish site at *http://world.altavista.com/* and try the online translation service there. The site will cope with English to Japanese, Chinese and Korean among other languages.

For Arabic translation you will probably need a software package. The £99 Al-Wafi product offers English to Arabic translation, although you will need to run it under the Arabic version of Windows. Find out more at *http://atasoft.com/products/wafi_v2.htm*. Be aware, though, that machine translations are rudimentary to say the least.

Q **I seem to have lost the built-in thesaurus from my copy of Microsoft Word, is there a stand-alone version I can use instead?**

A You should be able to reinstall the thesaurus by inserting your Microsoft CD. To choose the reinstall components option, check your product manual for details. Failing that, go to *www.wordweb.co.uk/free/* for the brilliant free Wordweb thesaurus and dictionary. It's a large download but it integrates nicely into Word and contains more than 120,000 root words. For real wordsmiths, the Pro version has anagrams, crossword pattern matching and user tailorable dictionaries for $18.

Q **I have some photos I took during the Second World War that are showing signs of age. Can you suggest software to produce copies that is simple enough for an old codger of 79?**

A There are a huge number of photo retouching packages available, but whether they can be classed as easy to use is another matter. My current favourite is Photolightning from *www.photolightning.com/*. This $39.95 program contains everything you will need to view, improve and print out your photographs, and it is probably as easy as any you will find at the moment. You will, of course, need a scanner to get your photographs into the computer before you begin.

Q **Please can you tell this aged computer user how to use Adobe Acrobat so I can download and use an instruction manual from a website?**

A Pop along to the *www.acrobat.com* site and click on the Get Acrobat Reader icon at the bottom right of the page to download the free software. Make a note of the download location on your hard disk and once the download has finished go there via My Computer and double click on the file name to install the reader. From then on, the reader will start up automatically when you access any Adobe PDF files on the web or on your computer.

Q **Is there any software or website which can be used to classify and catalogue a personal library of books?**

A There are several library packages around but one of the best I've seen is the $24.95 Book Library shareware from *www.wensoftware.com/*. It has a nice design and lets you add scanned images of the book cover as well as the usual bookworm type information. A free version limited to 50 books is available for online download and the company also supplies recipe and music versions.

Q **My Freecell card game has suddenly stopped working in Windows. I know it sounds frivolous but I miss it. Can you help?**

A A common and tricky problem, and not so frivolous since this is the most popular computer game in the world. Difficulties can arise because of a clash with Internet Explorer version 6.0, some anti-virus software or another computer component. Fear not though, you can find excellent free card game packages which include Freecell to download from *www.123freesolitaire.com* and *www.smaniac.com/sc.htm*.

Q **Please can you recommend some cheap software that lets you create your own web photo gallery?**

A Diji Album lets you take all your digital images and combine them with sound and visuals in a variety of album formats. You can create auto running CD albums to hand to friends and relatives, export the album to a web format for posting on the internet or simply email a compressed file to your nearest and dearest. The best thing about it though is that it's really easy to use. Just follow the wizard, as Judy Garland nearly sang long ago. It costs around £19 and a free trial is available for download from *www.xequte.com*.

Q **Is it possible to lock individual file folders so other people cannot have access to them but still have use of my computer?**

A You need the Hide Folders utility costing $24.95 from FS Pro Labs (*www.fspro.net*) which lets you lock and hide folders at will. This Windows program is simple to use and will also stop people inadvertently deleting your important folders. The free version lets you lock one folder, the paid for Pro and XP versions give you control of up to 64, plus password protection.

Q Do you know where I could get hold of an Irish family tree software package for my iMac?

A Holder of the Apple Mac genealogical software crown seems to be a program called Reunion (*www.leisterpro.com/*). I can't vouch for the intricacies of the program, but judging by the specifications it does everything except find those long lost 13th-century love letters in the attic. To focus on the Emerald Isle visit */www.rootsweb.com/~irish/*, which has a feast of Irish ancestral information.

Q I use an old 16bit version of a marine navigation software package which has just moved up to 32bit format. Why am I being forced to upgrade?

A This, I'm afraid, is the price of technological progress. Software developers say they need to keep advancing their products because of the increased power and features of today's hardware, and hardware makers talk about their own competitive pressures. I suspect that, in reality, most technological advances now occur simply because they can. The geeks are on a crusade and woe betide the pedestrians.

Q I am studying for a degree and have read about a software program which can help with essay planning. Can you help me locate it?

A The $14.95 Writing Tutor CD ROM, which you can order via mail order at *www.homeschooldiscount.com/home2/SSwriting.htm*, may be suitable, although it does look very US oriented. Have a look also at Power Write at *www.furman.edu/~moakes/Powerwrite/index.htm*, a detailed online writing tutorial from Furman University which seems quite impressive. Microsoft Word, by the way, includes a nice little outliner (as well as a grammar checker) which can help in the actual composition of your writing. Visit *www.outliners.com* for an overview of the technology.

Q I would like to be able to create maps. Can you recommend a cheap and easy cartography package?

A I suggest you explore Mr Odden's excellent resource on all things map-like at *http://oddens.geog.uu.nl/index.html*. Also take a look at the Versamap software from *www.versamap.com* or Ocad from *www.ocad.com*. The last two offer early versions as freeware, which is a nice touch I wish other developers would copy.

Q Someone in the school where I teach has altered the new document settings in Word so every new document we open contains some unwanted text. How can we make it revert to the original blank state?

A Somebody has been fiddling with your dot file settings, which are the templates which Word uses to define particular document types. Simply open up the file Normal.dot (File – Open – choose Files of Type dot then select), remove the offending text and save the file again with nothing in it. From then on you should be fine.

Q I recently downloaded a new web browser and now when I double click on my JPEG files it loads up instead of the photo editing software I use. How can I revert to the proper behaviour?

A The browser has muscled in and taken over your photo file associations so it can display them as needed. A quick way to sort this out is to download the 30-day free trial shareware Desktop Referee (*http://mc1soft.com/mcref.htm*), which lets you assign your own file associations and save them at will. The $14.95 program also lets you set up a permanent guard to prevent this happening again.

Q My father uses Lotus word processing software and cannot read the Word attachments he is sent via email. Is there any way to read these documents without having to buy the full Word program?

A Your dad needs the Microsoft Word viewer which is available for free download from the Microsoft site at *http://office.microsoft.com/officeupdate/*. Once he has installed this, he will be able to access any Word .doc file perfectly. Note, however, that he will not be able to edit or alter the documents, just read them.

Q **Is there such a thing as a directory of computer file types, to help identify what a PC file is for?**

A Getting to grips with file types, and in particular their extensions such as .zip, .exe or .jpeg, is certainly a good way of learning more about your PC workings. In fact, many PC problems occur because people delete files they shouldn't while doing a spot of spring cleaning. The index at *www.ace.net.nz/tech/TechFileFormat.html* contains a comprehensive listing of most of the known file types around at the moment. Best rule to remember is if in doubt, don't delete.

8 · Digital photography and mobile phones

Nowadays you can't walk 20 feet down a high street without stumbling across a mobile phone shop and every child demands a digital camera almost as soon as they can utter their first words. 'Mama…want Nikon,' they say.

As with all fashionable products, of course, there are pluses and minuses. The positives are that we all now have the tools to stay in touch wherever we are located and can record every living moment for posterity. The negatives are, of course, the same.

Two things are for sure, though: if it can get smaller, it will, and not every specification is necessarily a friendly specification. The mega manufacturing outlets in the Far East have become adept at churning out clone products with impressive feature lists – cameras with many, many megapixels, phone handsets with glamorous fashion specs. But beware: in many cases what the product carries in features it misses in build quality. And you, the unsuspecting buyer on the look out for a bargain, can be caught in the trap.

Top Don't Panic digital device tips

So what if it's obsolete

Let's be brutal shall we? Your brand new sparkly digital toy
is obsolete by the time you unpack it. The people who sold it
to you know the next model is in the testing phase back at
the factory in Kuala Lumpur and will really knock your
socks off when it arrives here in a few months. This is a fact
of our 21st-century digital life, I'm afraid, so live with it.
Enjoy the toy you have, get as much out of it as you can, and
let tomorrow's toys come when they will.

Specification isn't everything

Do specifications count? Absolutely. Are they all important?
Not as much as the salesmen would like us to think. The key
to buying well in the digital world is to ensure the product
has a proper balance between features, build quality and what I
like to call 'smarts'. Smarts are the subtle things which make a
product a pleasure to use rather than just a tool: a clever scroll
wheel, a simple menu structure, even a perfect size and pleasant
form. The best digital devices combine all three. Just look at the
Apple iPod or the Casio Exilim. If you simply choose on price
or specifications, you are doomed to a life of disappointment,
as anyone who has bought a super cheap, no-name four
megapixel digital camera from the Far East will tell you.

Don't skimp on batteries

It's surprising how little attention we pay to the batteries which power our portable devices, despite being a vital part of the equation. Modern batteries such as Li-Ion do not suffer from memory effect (where they gradually fail to hold charge after a while) but they do have a finite lifespan. So it is better to charge up only when you have to, rather than every time you pass a power socket. That way you help maximise the life of the cells. Be careful also when buying replacements. Cheap clones are common, but look closely at the specifications and you will notice they rarely hold as much charge as the branded versions, meaning quicker discharges. Sometimes the shoddy manufacturing can also result in hidden dangers – cheap exploding mobile phone batteries are not an uncommon event in the Far East.

The benefits of compromise

I'm often asked whether all-in-one products are better than individual devices which focus on one task. There is generally a compromise in quality with all-in-one PDAs or mobile phones but, at the end of the day, you have to decide whether the ease of having just one product to carry around outweighs any deficiency in features or performance. I personally enjoy having a Siemens SX1 mobile phone which can do duty as a camera, radio, music player and e-book reader, but others may prefer to buy better quality products for each purpose. Do try and test these products out before you buy to avoid disappointment later.

Top Don't Panic digital device questions

Q Can you recommend a good digital camera with a zoom feature at an affordable price?

A The key word here is 'affordable' because one man's cheap is, of course, another person's clutch-at-the-throat strangled gasp. Digital cameras have been steadily reducing in price and increasing in quality since they were launched, but they still have a way to go. The very cheapest digital models are really only useful for rudimentary photography and you need to spend £200 plus before the format starts offering decent features and picture quality. I quite like Kodak's EasyShare DX range, which is compact, flexible and offers a reasonable zoom and battery life. I also like its printer dock concept, which lets you print out photos instantly. Check out the current prices at online emporia such as *www.internetcamerasdirect.co.uk*.

Q I have taken movie clips with my digital camera, but they are in portrait mode which is difficult to view on my computer. How can I change them to landscape?

A How easy it is to forget that computer movie playing software will not rotate clips like normal photographs. The solution is to visit *www.virtualdub.com* to download and install the free VirtualDub program. Select Video – Filters – Add Filter and choose Rotate. Voila.

Q I am thinking of buying a digital camera but am worried about breaking it. Are there any robust models available?

A All modern gizmos are vulnerable if handled roughly and digital cameras are no exception. However, most of the better metal-bodied models are sturdy enough to survive a bit of rough and tumble – the Canon Ixus or the FujiFilm FinePix models, for example. You'll find a good selection which you can try out at any Jessops store (*www.jessops.com*).

In general, be careful with the lens and LCD screen and avoid sand, sea and cider spills. For a well-laid-out guide to digital camera buying and comprehensive reviews, visit the Digital Camera HQ at *www.digitalcamera-hq.com*.

Q Which is the safer method for archiving my digital photographs, CD or DVD?

A CDs are perfectly adequate for storing photos, although I prefer to use CD-R rather than CD-RW disks to make sure they are compatible with all computer drives. However, if you have the budget, go for a multiformat DVD recorder since they can store much more per disk and allow you to view photos on your DVD player and TV.

Q Is there a program that will let me capture photographs from my digital camera's movie clips?

A Pop over to *www.hypersnap.com* and download a test version of the HyperSnap-DX software. This super £20 utility for Windows will let you capture just about anything you see on your computer screen, including video and animation stills and even long, complex web pages.
For movie clip images, you need to enable the Special Capture feature then save in any of the normal formats for storing images.

Q I am in the market for a digital camera with the equivalent of 35mm quality. What number of pixels do I need?

A Digital camera quality revolves around much more than just pixel count. The quality of the optics, software and the camera's overall electronic design also play a vital role.
To obtain near 35mm quality you will probably need to spend around £1,500 right now, although prices are falling. For two highly rated and affordable options check out the Canon EOS 300D and the Nikon D70 digital SLRs in the excellent digicam review section at *www.dpreview.com/*.

Q I have been given a digital camera but the manual is totally inadequate. Is there anywhere I can go to learn more about its capabilities?

A For an in-depth appraisal of your camera's features, visit *www.imaging-resource.com* and do a search by make and model. A good general book on the subject is Digital Photography by Steve Bavister, which contains lots of helpful pictures and no-nonsense advice. I would also recommend The Complete Photography Manual edited by Ailsa McWhinnie, which has a digital section but, above all, offers great advice on all aspects of taking better snaps.

Q I am thinking of purchasing a digital camera in the US. Will I be able to show the pictures on my computer in this country without having to purchase additional equipment?

A The main problem is that the power supply for the camera may not be useable in the UK unless you buy a universal voltage model. As long as the camera captures the digital photos in a standard format such as JPEG you should be fine with editing and viewing your photos on a UK-bought PC. Note that this does not apply to camcorders which typically use one or other of the mutually incompatible PAL and NTSC video formats. Don't forget if you buy abroad you may have difficulty finding warranty support.

Q I keep hearing about something called SMS. What is it and how can I use it?

A SMS stands for Short Message Service and is basically a method of sending text messages from one mobile phone to another in much the same way as PC to PC email. Short means you can't send more than 160 characters at a time, but despite this limitation the service is one of the most popular parts of the mobile phone revolution. Youngsters, in particular, use it all the time to chat about this and that, and up to 15 billion messages a month are currently flowing around the world's cellular network.

Q Is it possible to use a moble phone to get on the internet at a reasonable speed? I have tried and seem to be restricted to a fax speed of 9.5kbps.

A Current mobile phone technology was never designed for moving data around and, consequently, has a speed limit of 9,600 bits per second (bps), around five times slower than a conventional modem. The new Generalised Packet Radio Service (GPRS) is up and running and promises to make accessing the web less like watching paint dry. The good news is that GPRS works in many different countries; the bad is that its download speeds of around 50kbps (close to home modems) will still seem painfully slow because of the paltry processing power of today's mobile handsets.

Q I have just purchased a laptop to take abroad but there is no landline at the property we are renting. Can I access the internet using a mobile phone?

A Your best bet is either to use a laptop-to-phone cable connection kit (examples can be found at *www.mobiles.co.uk/datacables.html*) or pick up a Xircom Bluetooth PC card laptop adapter for around £100 and use it with one of the new Bluetooth enabled phones such as the Ericsson T610. With the right phone an infra-red connection, although tricky, is also a possibility. Check out more detailed instructions at *http://homepages.tesco.net/~hcsc/irgsmmobiles.htm*.

Q Is there any way to send SMS messages to a mobile phone using the internet and a PC or Macintosh?

A There are a number of free SMS services offered on the world wide web – check out the list from TextMeFree at *www.textmefree.com/UK_Only/You* sign up online, enter the destination phone number and the message and press send. Many services are free at the moment, so you may have to suffer all sorts of advertising, but you save money as well as avoid having to fiddle with those diddy keys on your mobile phone.

Q **Can I collect my Hotmail messages on my Orange SPV smart phone?**

A Hotmail operates a specialised server to deliver email to Outlook Express, which is something your phone does not support. It is probably only a matter of time before this kind of direct downloading comes to phones, but until then, Hotmail can be accessed through the phone's web browser or with the special mobile email delivery service offered by Microsoft at *http://mobile.msn.com*.

Q **Can you recommend a pay-as-you-go SIM card for our mobile phones while on holiday in America?**

A Phoning in the US can become a tad expensive with your UK mobile phone. It can prove cheaper to buy a native SIM card upon arrival to benefit from cheaper calls. Of course, this means putting up with a new phone number for the duration of your trip, but for many people the savings outweigh the inconvenience. The best idea is to find a mobile phone shop at your destination, but for those who would rather go forearmed, you can buy roaming SIM cards from *www.orate.co.uk/Roaming/Index.html* before departing. The phone must be unlocked to accept these.

Q Can I have football results delivered to my mobile phone?

A The airwaves are awash with football scores as companies mine the gold between the goalposts. Most service providers offer football or sports results. One of the best is Vodafone's Footie on the Fone (*www.vizzavi.co.uk/uk/alertsfootie.html*) and *The Sunday Times* Goals Flash service can be set up by telephoning 0870 900 8672 from your mobile.

Q I am trying to back up my mobile phone contacts with Nokia's PC Suite software, but it keeps failing despite trying different computers. Can you help?

A It sounds as though either your cable or your handset connector is faulty. Beware of cheap unbranded cables, as they can be a false economy. Take the handset and cable to a phone repair shop and see if it can test them. Failing that, try one of the new SIM card back-up products, such as the Texet Simkey £14.99 from *www.iwantoneofthose.com*. Simply slot in your SIM card and copy the information across for safekeeping. Alternatively, *www.phonesaved.com* will back up a phone's address book over the airwaves.

Q **Can I forward mobile phone voicemail messages to my email account?**

A Most mobile phone networks can provide text or email notification of incoming voicemail. However to hear the message itself, you will need a service that will accept a forwarded voice message, attach it to an email and send it to your specified address. One example can be found at *www.callagenix.com/services/brochure.htm*. Sadly, speech-recognition systems are not yet good enough to transcribe the audio to text, so the message will arrive as a bulky audio attachment.

Q **What is the best way to transfer photos from my computer to the handset of a Sony Ericsson mobile phone?**

A My advice is to stay away from Bluetooth for now because of some remaining inter-operability problems and opt for infra-red. Hold the phone about six inches from your computer's infra-red port, with the two dark red windows facing each other. If you are running Windows XP, the computer should 'see' the phone automatically; if you don't have infra-red on your computer, you can buy a small USB adaptor at *www.logomanager.co.uk*.

Q What is the best way to back-up and synchronise my mobile phone calendar and contact information with my PC?

A Take a look at MightyPhone (*www.mightyphone.com*). This online service automatically updates your address books, calendars, notes and tasks from phone to web or phone to PC. The Pro version will also synchronise appointments between your phone and Microsoft Outlook. You will need a SyncML-capable phone, and a year's subscription costs £39.99 if you buy via your local Carphone Warehouse outlet.

Q Is there a handheld device that incorporates email, radio, digital camera, phone and internet?

A Take a look at the new Siemens SX1 phone (*www.my-siemens.co.uk*). I've been playing with one for a while and it really seems worth the price (from about £155 with contract). It has an excellent colour screen and fun functions, such as an integrated FM radio, an MP3 player and a camera, yet it is small enough to be used as a standard phone. Though the keypad layout is bizarre, it has one of the most impressive arrays of features on the market. You can find it at *www.expansys.com/product.asp?code=SX1* or on your nearest high street.

Q I have recently been given a mobile phone with my new job and was wondering if there is a way to divert the calls from my old phone?

A All you have to do is set up a call divert on your phone – usually by accessing the Call Divert function in the phone's menu and set to Divert All Calls without Ringing. Enter in the destination phone number and you should be all set. Note that you will be paying the onward portion of the call from your old phone to the new phone, so you will probably want to get callers to ring you back on the new number sharpish.

Q Does it harm my mobile phone to keep charging the battery every day?

A The charging and use of modern batteries is a complex subject because of the different types on the market. Early NiCad (nickel cadmium) batteries suffered from what is known as memory effect and could very quickly lose their capacity to hold a charge if you kept charging them when it wasn't necessary. Later versions though, such as NiMH (nickel metal hydride) and Li-Ion (lithium ion), do not have this problem. They are often referred to as 'smart' batteries because they are much better at handling partial charging and discharging cycles. Visit *http://michaelbluejay.com/batteries/* for more information.

Q I remember seeing a report suggesting mobile phone hands-free kits were not as safe as many thought. Is that true?

A The Consumers' Association did indeed find that hands-free kits – or to be more precise the two kits it tested which 'consumers commonly purchase' – could increase rather than decrease the effective radiation levels of phones at the user's head. This is clearly just one test and more work needs to be done. I will, however, simply restate the government sponsored Stewart Report on mobile phones which said: 'The gaps in knowledge are sufficient to justify a precautionary approach.'

Q I keep hearing the term 3G mentioned in connection with mobile phones. What does it mean exactly?

A This service (otherwise known as third generation) promises to deliver all sorts of wonderful information and entertainment across the cellular network to mobile phones and wireless devices such as palmtop computers. Regrettably, it appears the cellular service providers have spent so much on their government 3G licences that the poor old consumer will need to fork out huge subscription fees to access the service. I suspect this will eventually lead to a lot of gripe, gripe, gripe.

Q I am coming up to the end of my annual mobile phone contract. Is it easy to change to a pay-as-you-go service and can I keep my old number?

A Changing service providers at the end of your contract is a simple matter. First notify your existing supplier by phone or in writing that you want to cancel and then take a trip to your local mobile phone shop to buy a pay-as-you-go SIM pack. Note that you may need to pay a small transfer fee if you're changing providers.

However, my friends at Oftel tell me there should be no phone unlocking fee payable after 12 months is up, and if you change suppliers you have the right to take your number with you. To take your old number, get a PAC (porting authorising code) from your old supplier, give it to your new one and it will do the transfer in around a week.

Q **As a football manager I need to contact my players on a weekly basis. Calling their mobiles is very costly so I prefer to send text messages from my PC. Can I do this to them all simultaneously?**

A What you really need, apart from some penetrating crosses from the right wing, is SMS Centre (*www.5star-shareware.com/Internet/SMS/sms-centre.html*). This £25 software program lets you send those all-important SMS messages from your PC to any pre-defined group of users. The product can also be used to send messages to pagers and uses standard Windows PC modems or an ISDN line. For an extra £12 you can add an email plug-in which will forward POP3 email messages from your PC to any mobile phone or pager. Definitely a better bargain than a new European striker.

Q **Will I be able to use my mobile phone in the US when I travel there later this year?**

A Only if it supports the GSM 1900 frequency. The US is slowly adopting the worldwide GSM standard, but for some strange reason it originally decided to use a different handset

frequency to the rest of us. The result is that you need
a special dual or tri-band phone which will work over here
and in the US. You will also need a service provider with
access in the area you are visiting. Don't forget to switch on
your international roaming service before you go either.
Call your service provider for details.

Q What can I do with redundant mobile phones? I have a
collection of three so far (all without SIM cards) as a result of
upgrading. Can they be recycled somehow?

A Eurosource (*www.esel.co.uk/*) operates a phone and
inkjet cartridge recycling service in conjunction with schools
and charities, so it may be worth giving it a call on 0845 130
20 10. Otherwise, try Cellular Reclamation (*www.cellular-
rec.co.uk/*) which operates a scheme linked with the Water
Aid charity.

Q Is it true that I have to pay the call charges on incoming
calls when using my mobile phone abroad on holiday?

A Roaming mobile phone charges are a well-kept secret.
I was astonished on my first trip to the US with a Cellnet
mobile to find I was being charged international rates for
a portion of all incoming calls to my voice mail and phone.
This is standard practice, so I suggest switching off your

phone (and voice mail divert) while abroad unless it's essential or you fancy the dangerous thrill of opening the phone bill on your return.

Q What exactly is a WAP phone and should I get one?

A WAP phones are mobile handsets designed to access the internet. At one point it was believed they were designed by a geek comic solely to induce hysterical laughter, since they seldom seemed to do anything except sit there struggling to connect. However, recent developments suggests WAP technology may eventually end up being quite useful. WAP services can deliver everything from sports results to location information to your mobile, so you could find it helpful if you're an Arsenal-supporting business executive who always needs to know where the nearest Starbucks is.

Q I have been told it is easier to create SMS text messages on a mobile phone that uses predictive text. What does this mean exactly?

A Most handsets use a system called T9 predictive text to provide an easier means of inputting words into messages. This software makes an intelligent guess as to the word you're trying to write and fills it in for you as you hit the keys. As a result, you only have to tap the letter keys once instead of a number of times. The secret to using the system, by the way, is not to look at the screen until you have finished typing the word. For a good demo tutorial visit *www.t9.com*.

Q If I buy a new mobile phone will I be able to use my existing SIM card?

A You can transfer SIM cards from phone to phone provided they support the same type of mobile service. So if you have a Vodafone account and buy a new phone, you will be able to transfer the card as long as the new phone supports Vodafone or O2 (which operate using the same frequency). It is a similar story with T-Mobile, Orange and Virgin, which share the same type of phones. The matter is complicated a tad by the fact that many modern phones are dual mode and so will cope with different standards automatically. Note that certain suppliers are now rather sneakily locking phones to their service, so if you buy a second-hand phone you may have to pay an 'unlocking' fee so it can use another service's compatible SIM card.

Q Can you tell me if there is a mobile phone that can send and receive email with ease, or is it only possible with a combination of mobile phone and PDA?

A I generally don't like saying wait a while as something better will come along soon, but in this case it's a sensible option. At the moment we are in transition between the old-style basic mobile phones and the new generation of smartphones, which will handle email, internet and even

photo taking without breaking stride. The Nokia 6600 and
the Sony Ericsson P900 are two current products which
spring to mind in this regard.

Q **How can I tell what is the best quality digital camera to buy?**

A Digital cameras come in all sorts of shapes, sizes and
qualities. The thing that most people check is the pixel count
of the camera (eg 1.5 megapixel) which gives an indication
of how clear and sharp the pictures are likely to be and what
size you will be able to print out. However there are other
important issues. Some of the best value cameras may not
have the largest pixel count but offer great optics and lenses,
a long battery life and cool features such as swivel mount
lenses. Nikon, FujiFilm, Canon and Olympus are probably
the most popular brands at the moment, although they tend to
sit at the pricier end of the market.

9 · Home technology

Home entertainment used to mean a colour telly, a record
player and a radio alarm in the bedroom, but suddenly,
here at the start of the 21st century, things have changed.
The experts talk of convergence and home automation and
other such grand ideas, but for most of us this ends up
meaning too many cables, complicated installation
instructions and not enough hours in the day to program
the date into the VCR.

The truth is that home electronics are really only just
starting to come into their own, and over the coming years
we will witness a veritable revolution in the living room.
Products like personal video recorders (sometimes known as
digital video recorders), internet connected appliances
including fridges and washing machines and, of course,
automated systems which govern everything from our central
heating to our alarm clock are lurking in the wings just
waiting to amaze us.

Of course, there's likely to be a lot of frustration riding
along with all the glitter, and that's where Don't Panic
comes in.

Top Don't Panic home technology tips

Box clever with upgrades

The centrepiece of most people's home entertainment is still the television set, and nowhere is the digital revolution happening faster than in respect of the humble box. After decades of stagnation, the TV is morphing into a super surround sound, widescreen, cinema-like phenomenon – and that's just the beginning. The main reason for upgrading, apart from keeping up with the Joneses down the road, is to get the best out of the new raft of broadcast services.

We are about to enjoy the fruits of interactive services, movies on demand, multi camera angle broadcasts and beyond, and it pays to consider upgrading now to be ready. Remember also that the government plans to switch off old-style analogue services sometime within the next five years to make way for more efficient digital broadcast services, so change is inevitable.

Be wireless savvy

It can be difficult to cope with the proliferation of cables as more electronic products make their way into our living rooms, and for this reason many people are looking at wireless technologies. There are two issues to consider here. First, be sure you have a home that is sufficiently wireless friendly to make the switch worthwhile. Despite the advertising claims, many wireless technologies don't work well through multiple thick walls beyond 50 or 80 feet. And try not to mix and match too many wireless technologies in one location. They are supposed to be fully compatible but there are instances where they can clash if frequencies overlap, even with their clever switching systems.

Be power conscious

Electronic devices use power, and the more you have in your home, the more juice they will need. You can minimise the drain (and your electricity bill) by following a couple of simple rules. Make sure you switch off all non-essential equipment when possible. Leaving a device on standby still consumes power, and if you have a lot humming away you will be using a fair amount of electricity. Also try to buy wisely. Most of the larger electrical appliances now come with power use ratings, so go for those with the best consumption values. An A-rated product is much more efficient than an E-rated one and will save you money over time.

Update your formats

Equipment inevitably wears out or becomes obsolete and you can be left with a mountain of old data on strange formats. VHS and Betamax tapes, 8mm movie tape and the cassette format spring to mind. Ensure you copy important material onto new media as soon as you can, either using any of the agencies that exist for the purpose or your own cable and box solution. I recently discovered a load of old reel-to-reel tape which was on the verge of disintegrating and it was only through some quick legwork that I managed to save the material to CD in time. Don't be caught out by the march of progress!

Top Don't Panic home technology questions

Q I have a JVC television that can accept surround-sound speakers but I would prefer to avoid a mess of cabling. Are any wireless speakers available?

A I suspect more marital strife has been caused by snaking cables, ugly speakers and stacks of set-top boxes than by any other home technology. You can avoid at least one of those tiffs by purchasing Philex Pulsar 3000 wireless speakers (*www.beststuff.co.uk/philex_pulsar_3000.htm*). These £99 units won't please real audiophiles, as the sound quality is inevitably degraded without wires, but they should be fine for rear auxiliary speakers, to give you that 'immersed' feel.

Q What are the best options for upgrading my VHS recorder?

A I would wait for the next generation of personal video recorders (PVRs), which combine hard disk and DVD recording in one convenient package. These superhero boxes will also access the all-important electronic programme guides, allowing you to select essential viewing a week or two ahead. Philips and Panasonic will be releasing models over the coming months. They may be pricey at first but you will be able to automatically record a whole season of a series, for example, so you need never miss your favourite programmes because of an impromptu night out.

Also check out the new £250 twin-tuner Digifusion FVRT100 digital video recorder (*www.fusiondigitec.com/files/newsite/consumer_prods/ uk_available_now/FVRT100/fvrt100*), which allows you to record Freeview digital programmes onto its hard disk via a seven-day on-screen channel guide.

Q **I recently bought an American DVD that will not work in my player because it is for the wrong region. What can I do?**

A You can overcome the nasty regional grinch if your DVD player can be set to multi-region with a special remote control code. Visit *www.dvd.reviewer.co.uk/info/multiregion* to see if your model is featured. If not, I am afraid you have just bought a nice drinks coaster, unless you have a DVD drive in your computer and a copy of DVD Region-Free (£24 from *www.dvdidle.com*).

Q **Are there any televisions on which you can set a maximum volume, thus avoiding the adverts being louder than the programmes?**

A Commercials are not actually louder than the programmes, but because of the way the audio signal is sometimes compressed during adverts, giving less variation between loud and quiet than in ordinary programmes, our ears perceive them as louder. If you still want to set a maximum volume, have a wander round your local electrical goods retailers and look out for some of the newer television sets, for example the Sony models with Steady Sound Automatic Volume Control. Your ears will thank you, not to mention your neighbours.

Q Is it possible to set up a webcam to monitor my home while I am away on holiday?

A With the right type of motion detection software, such as Stealth Big Brother (the Gold Edition costs £50 from *www.easylife.co.uk*), you can set up a rudimentary webcam system to keep tabs on anyone roaming about the house, but this means leaving your computer running. An alternative is Video Mark VCR Commander (£153 from *www.cyberselect.co.uk*) which detects motion and records colour footage onto your VCR. For a really cut-price solution visit *www.mobcam.cz* and download the free MobCam software for Symbian smartphones.

Q There is sand in my portable CD player and it now refuses to work. Is it salvageable?

A If the sand was wet and salty, some corrosion may occur if the affected parts are not dried and cleaned quickly. Do not power up the machine until you are sure it is completely dry. A local repair shop may help, but if not, use a hairdryer on a low heat to dry the sand and a small vacuum-cleaner attachment to suck it out. Visit *http://repairfaq.ece.drexel.edu/REPAIR/* for more detailed help.

Q **My Betamax video recorder has broken and I have hundreds of tapes recorded in the format. Is there anywhere that will fix it?**

A Palsite Info (*www.palsite.info/directory.html*) has information on all sorts of video-recording paraphernalia, including a section on Betamax repairers and places that sell second-hand models in case yours is beyond repair. Also try *www.loot.com* or *www.ebay.co.uk*, which often have used machines for sale. Do search the web for video-tape conversion services, though, as the supply of repairers and machines will dry up eventually.

Q **I recently bought a double CD album that will not play on any of our stereo systems, even after obtaining a replacement. What is going on?**

A This sounds like a copy-protected CD, though a better word is corrupted. You can find a list of such broken albums on Fat Chuck's site at *http://www.fatchuck.com/z3.html* or at *http://ukcdr.org/issues/cd/bad*. Philips, a founder of the CD standard, has warned the record labels that these disks are not CDs at all and should, therefore, carry warning stickers outlining the dangers of purchase. Caveat emptor! Also beware that enhanced or super audio CDs may not work in ordinary players.

Q **Are 'Carrier Pre-Select' phone companies a good alternative to BT?**

A CPS services automatically route calls to a selected carrier without having to dial special numbers or install boxes. Using this kind of service you should find the carrier's rates are better than BT's. Try the excellent service at *www.uswitch.com* to find a suitable carrier, or the comprehensive telephone tariff list at *www.magsys.co.uk/telecom/residx.htm*. Keep your bifocals close by, though, as there is masses of small print.

Q **Can I listen to my computer stored music collection through my stereo system without running cables across the house?**

A The Wireless Exstreamer from the Swiss company Barix (£206 from *www.laser.com/* will beam audio from a computer to a stereo system. It is not the prettiest box in the world, but it does have some quite sophisticated components.

Q Will my camcorder tapes be wiped by the x-ray machine at the airport?

A Your tapes should be fine going through the machines. I have taken many mini DV camcorder holiday tapes through security checks at airports and have never had a problem – though my long-suffering family probably wish I had. The British Airports Authority recommends putting tapes or undeveloped camera film in hand luggage rather than suitcases destined for the hold, where stronger scanners are used. Digital camera memory cards should also pass through the scanners without being wiped. For more information, see the Travel Tips sections (under each airport's Travel Guide) at *www.baa.co.uk*.

Q We are travelling to Canada and want to buy a portable DVD player to keep the children occupied during the trip. What should we watch out for?

A Portable DVD players have, fortunately, started to decrease in price and can now be found for about £200 – visit *www.allcam.biz/products/ptdvd.html* for a couple of multi-region players. The big consideration, apart from what films to watch, is battery life. Check the model you buy offers enough to view a whole film – or be prepared for tears before bedtime. It may be wise to buy a spare battery and keep it fully charged.

Q Whenever the central heating is on the picture on my digital television disintegrates. What could be the problem?

A It sounds as though you are a victim of wideband impulsive noise. No, that is not the children clattering around in the hallway, but electrical interference caused by anything from a hairdryer to a loose wire in a plug or socket. The most likely cause of your problem is a badly suppressed or ageing thermostat – even those located in a neighbour's home can have an effect. Further details and a simple interference test can be found at
www.ofcom.org.uk/static/archive/ra/rahome.htm.

Q Are some DVD films encrypted so they will not play in a multi-region machine?

A Regional Code Enhanced (RCE) disks are not actually encrypted, but you need to check the player is set for the same region as the disk. If the regions clash (as can happen with multi-region machines) the disk will not play. Not all disks are RCE enabled but you can overcome the problem if you find one. For more information go to *www.dvdtalk.com/rce.html*. RCE beating players are also available at *www.codefreedvd.com*.

Q I want to put my cassette and vinyl collection onto CD but need to run a 30-foot cable to connect my computer to the hi-fi system. Will this be a problem?

A It depends how important top quality reproduction is to your ears. Longer cables can result in some high frequency loss, hum and increased noise. However, 30 feet is not that far and with good quality shielded cable and connectors, the sound should be fine. Generally, it is better to move the two components closer together.

Q We have bought a new flat without an external television aerial. Is there any service that will provide a good picture?

A Your first port of call should be the cable providers, but failing that, try a terrestrial digital set-top box with signal boosting SetPal technology – visit *www.radioandtelly.co.uk/freeviewreceivers.html* for a selection. These boxes do a good job of improving weaker digital signals such as you might get with an indoor aerial. Ultimately, your picture quality will depend on how far you are from the transmitter and whether there are any obstructions in the path of the signal. A good indoor aerial with signal booster will also help (see *www.argos.co.uk*). If all else fails, wave the aerial around a little until the fuzz clears.

Q I recently bought a radio controlled watch, but it does not appear to update the time when I travel abroad. Is it broken?

A Radio watches tune in to remote transmitters to keep constantly updated with the correct time. However, would-be time travellers should note not all such products are born equal. The cheaper ones access only UK transmitters so cannot update while you are abroad. Better models, such as Casio's WaveCeptor range (*www.casio.co.uk/timepiece/wristnetworks*), work with multiple transmitters here and on the Continent, which give automatic updated coverage.

Q Television broadcast audio seems to have improved recently. Is this because the channels are using Dolby sound?

A Conventional analogue broadcasts air mostly in Nicam stereo, while the digital channels, such as Freeview, transmit MPEG stereo. But the best sound comes from films transmitted on the Sky Plus system, which arrive in glorious Dolby Digital 5.1 surround. You will need to connect the Sky box to a 5.1 digital decoder and surround speakers to get the full effect, so be prepared to spend from £100 to £500 for the privilege of fully immersive sound.

Q Why does the output from my digital set-top box lag about two seconds behind my other analogue equipment?

A Blame MPEG compression. Compressed digital transmissions need to be decoded when they reach your home, this is what creates the lag. Put an old television next to a new digital one and you will notice the difference.

Q I'm thinking of buying a new video recorder and television. Are the ones which combine a VCR and TV in one box worth getting?

A Most people who buy a combo unit do so because they offer size and portability benefits. They are also easier to set up and use because of the all-in-one format – just shove a tape in the slot, select the AV channel and up comes the picture. You do lose on the flexibility, however, of choosing a higher grade VCR to go with your TV and vice versa. And perhaps most important, if the VCR goes wrong, the whole unit will have to be sent to the menders, which means no TV as well. The final point to note is that you will pay for the privilege of having one of these combination units and, in most cases, you can buy better quality separates for the same or lower price.

Q I have bought an integrated digital television. Is it possible to record the Freeview channels?

A Indeed it is. Attach the VCR to your television via the Scart 1 port and tune the recorder to the AV channel or an unused channel so you can see the output from the television. To record, select the digital channel you want on the television, switch to the AV or input channel you have set up for the VCR and press record. Note you will not be able to watch one channel while recording another, unless your digital box has two tuners.

Q **I recently upgraded to the Freeview digital television service but cannot locate a VCR with a digital tuner. Why?**

A The video cassette recorder is a dying breed and so is attracting little or no research investment. Television is in transition. Video on demand, time-shifting PVR machines and the changing face of 21st-century transmission and reception are transforming the landscape. Put any serious purchases on hold until the smoke has cleared and the analogue era has started to fade into a little white dot.

Q **I'd like to send a DVD of a TV series to my son in the US. Will a UK-bought DVD play on an American iMac computer?**

A DVDs are region coded. This means only those matching the region of the player can play on that device. The upshot is that UK disks – Region 2 – will not play on Region 1 US machines and vice versa. It's ridiculous and hugely unpopular but it's a fact of life for now thanks to the movie industry. Luckily, if you hunt around you can find region-free (also known as multi-region) players and computer drives everywhere. Check out *www.richersounds.co.uk* or *www.codefreedvd.com*.

Q We have a new flat which has been wired with Category 5 cabling. How can I use it?

A Cat 5 cabling, also known as structured cabling, has been developed to make it easy to pipe computer, video or audio feeds from room to room without having to pull up floorboards or the skirting each time. It accepts all the different makes of equipment and types of data without batting an eyelid, but the downside is that you need to learn about hubs and patch panels to be hip to the lingo. Check out *www.combsnet.com/cable/index.html* for a great primer on the subject.

Q Is it possible to play video CDs that I have created on my PC on my DVD player?

A This is a definite maybe. Recent model dual laser DVD players seem to play VCDs with no problem but earlier ones may not. It also seems to depend on the type of video CD disk you are using. Store bought movies – such as from *www.lala.co.uk* – will most likely play, while ones you create yourself may not, especially if you create them using CD-RW disks. The safe rule is that the newer the DVD player, the more likely it is to cope with video CDs.

Q Every day I get a fax from a company listing the latest exchange rates. I never asked to be put on its subscriber list so how can I get off it?

A Under the Telecommunications (Data Protection and Privacy) Regulations 1999 it is unlawful for companies to send faxes to an individual without prior consent, and companies risk a £5,000 fine if they continue harassing you. So subscribe to the Oftel sponsored Fax Preference Service (*www.fpsonline.org.uk/* or 020 7766 4420) where you can register an official complaint and receive help in dealing with unwanted spam contacts like this. Online registration is a real snap after which you will receive a letter of confirmation outlining your rights. You can also receive protection from junk telephone call abuse.

Beware though of opportunist companies which are sending out junk faxes offering to register you with the Fax Preference Service via an expensive premium rate phone number. The FPS is reviewing its procedures to see if it can prevent this type of thing in the future.

Q I am finding it very hard to locate a shop selling a microphone to record live singing and live music. Most stores sell them only for speech recording. Can you suggest where I can look?

A You need a professional recording shop or one that caters for the home studio enthusiast. The kind of microphones you are looking for range from around £100 to several thousand pounds, so they are not likely to be in your local Woolies. Try *www.audio-toyshop.co.uk* or *www.elmusic.co.uk*. The £80 Shure SM58 was a good all-round performer a while back, but you may find more contemporary models a better choice now.

Q When will mass market DVD recorders be available here?

A DVD recordable drives have started arriving on the market for PC and Apple computers. Pioneer, for example, has just released the DVR-A03 which will let you record onto standard DVD disks which can then be played on ordinary DVD machines in the home. The technology, however, is not 'finished' and prices need to come down a lot from the current £600 or so before we'll all rush out and buy one. Visit *www.pioneerdvdrw.co.uk* for more details.

Q Do you need a special receiver to access digital radio services? If so, is it worth the extra expense?

A You will indeed need a sparkly new receiver for the new DAB – or digital audio broadcasts – and you will find them in most reputable hi-fi emporia. DAB promises CD-quality radio transmissions free from interference caused by low flying mountains, high rise buildings or inclement weather. The sound is certainly better than conventional FM stereo under the right conditions, but the real benefit will be the addition of data transmission. Imagine being able to receive lyrics while a song plays, a biography of the performer or even having the opportunity to buy tickets for their next concert. Unfortunately, these services are not being delivered as quickly as originally promised, which, while typical of many new technology introductions, is a shame.

Q I would like to purchase a radio for use on the move but cannot find one that offers long wave which I like for sport. Can you help?

A If you have a nostalgic bent and plenty of cash, consider buying one of the lovely Roberts radios. They look and sound beautiful and are available in the UK from specialist retailers or from *www.ogormans.co.uk/roberts.htm*.

Q **What is the difference between infra-red cordless headphones and the new 864MHz FM wireless models?**

A The most noticeable difference is price, which basically reflects the different characteristics of the two products. Wireless infra-red headphones operate by 'line of sight', which means you have to be standing within view of the transmitter box to hear anything, while the more expensive radio FM versions will beam their signal through walls and floors up to the limit of their range. Don't expect outstanding sound quality from either though – in that respect you are still better off with conventional wired headphones like my beloved BeyerDynamic set.

Q **Many current digital camcorders have a two-way DV in/out recording port for transferring video material, but my Sony PC10 is a few years old and only has DV out. Is it possible to upgrade it to two way?**

A Sorry, but with this particular model the only way is by a hardware modification, and this is simply not feasible. Those with other digital camcorder models who want to make their DV ports two-way should, however, check out the Widget product from Datavision (*www.datavision.co.uk/*). Check your warranty terms first though.

Q I want to buy a digital TV package but am confused by all options on offer. Are there any sites where you can compare?

A A site which features a wealth of information on digital TV in the UK is at *www.digitalspy.co.uk/*. As well as containing network channel and pricing information, there's a discussion group where you can ask for advice from users and enthusiasts. For a price comparison on widescreen televisions try *http://uk.kelkoo.com*.

Q Is there such as thing as a stand-alone CD recorder which has two drives so you can play and record from one CD to another quickly and simply?

A The Phillips CDR 775 provides just such a dubbing feature, using twin CD decks and some cute electronics. Check out *www.srtl.co.uk/srtl/cdr775.html* for more details. You can also find it for sale online for around £180 in the electrical department at *www.amazon.co.uk*.

Q I would like to set up a home theatre with a flat-screen and sound system using only a DVD player and no television. Is this possible?

A Prepare to dig deep into those pockets for a flat-screen system to fit your bill. Several manufacturers now make LCD monitors which will accept high resolution input from stand-alone DVD players, but at a price. Check out the Sharp LC range at *www.techtronics.com/uk/shop/864-00-lcd-plasma-tv.html* to see what I mean.

Q I will be going to the Far East soon and was wondering if a mini disk Walkman bought over there would work in Ireland and if you'd recommend buying one.

A Walkmans by definition are portable battery powered units, so there's no obvious reason why a Far Eastern model wouldn't work in Ireland. The thing to remember, though, is that if anything goes wrong, you will be a long way from the shop where you bought it, and there's no guarantee a local store will be willing or able to fix it. It's an age-old conundrum: buy cheaper and take the risk or spend a bit extra and have more peace of mind? It's your call!

Q I have a vast vinyl collection and only one turntable to play it on. Is there such a thing as a compact record player that plugs straight into the mains and not via a hi-fi?

A Oh the lost days of the record player – Dansette (*www.dansettes.co.uk/*), Bush, Fidelity, crackle, hiss, pop, warble, scratch, alas no more. I'm afraid the glory days of the record player combo are well and truly over. However, as with all things, retro is making a comeback, so why not take a look at the £99.99 Roxy1 60s style player at *www.globalgadgetuk.com/interesting-items.htm?*

Q I have a Playstation 2. Can I connect it to my PC to watch DVDs and play games?

A PS2 consoles can be connected only to monitors that accept a composite SVideo or RF (television aerial) input. You may be able to fudge a solution using the RF input of a PC TV card, but the sound and video quality will suffer. You can, however, obtain better game graphics quality by hooking it up to your television with a proper Scart RGB cable (not the one supplied in the box). Note you will also get better DVD playback on your TV by using an S-Video cable out (via a Scart adapter if necessary) rather than the standard wire supplied in the PS2 box.

Q Where might I find a broadcast quality microphone for doing voice recording on my PC?

A Cheap microphones are definitely not to be recommended if you are going to do any proper recording, but there are a number of better quality microphones on the market for studio and live broadcast use. The Rode NT1A studio condenser microphone has been getting some excellent reports lately, both for its quality and for its competitive price. More information can be found at *www.soundslive.co.uk/moreinfo.asp?id=279*. Remember, though, that the sound you get will also depend on your environmental set up, so take time to sort out the acoustics.

Q **What should I look for if I want to buy a digital camcorder in the US?**

A I strongly suggest you do not risk buying a camcorder in the US unless you are sure the product will work properly in the UK. Apart from obvious problems such as differences in power supply requirements, there are incompatibilities between the PAL and NTSC TV output on either side of the Atlantic, as well as warranty and support considerations. Although there are ways around these issues, unless you are familiar with the differing technologies it may be better to steer well clear.

Q **I have a digital answering machine which works fine until I attach a modem to the line at which point it stops answering the phone as if it was switched off. What could be wrong?**

A There are two possibilities here. It could be a REN problem, which indicates you may have too many devices attached to your home's telephone line system. All the REN numbers together mustn't add up to more than four, and most modern devices have a REN of one or two. Try removing phones or devices and see if that stops the problem. Alternatively, your modem could be set to auto answer and be cutting in before the answering machine has a chance to do its work. Check your modem manual for the command to turn off auto answer and insert that in the box in Control Panel – Modems – Properties – Connection – Advanced – Extra Settings.

Q **Which technology offers better sound quality: super audio CD or DVD audio?**

A The consensus among the experts at the moment is that super CD just has the edge, although you'll probably need bat ears to tell the difference. My advice is to hold off from investing in either for a while until the threat of a standards war recedes and there is more content available on one or the other. If you're determined, though, you can splash out £200 on a Pioneer DV656K (*www.empiredirect.co.uk/index.asp*) which will play both.

Q **I am looking to buy a television and video package, should I buy online from the US as American prices tend to be lower?**

A Do not even consider buying this sort of equipment online from the US. For one thing, it is highly unlikely they will sell/ship it to you and, for another, even if they did it wouldn't work over here. American power and video transmission standards are completely different from ours. On the whole, stay away from buying electrical goods online from abroad unless you are familiar with the potential pitfalls.

Q **I am keen to buy a plasma television but am put off by the high price. Do any retailers offer a rental option and are prices likely to fall in the near future?**

A Plasma screens are expensive to produce because of the technology involved, so we are unlikely to see any significant price drop within the next few years. In terms of rental, your best bet is to look for a specialist supplier locally. You can rent them for professional use, but – are you sitting down? – this is likely to work out at around £170 or more a day.

Q **I recently bought a 28-inch widescreen television with Dolby Pro-logic and matching DVD player and video. If I wanted to connect an amplifier to the system would a normal mini hi-fi system do?**

A You can attach any conventional modern hi-fi system to your home cinema system, as long as both sides of the arrangement have compatible connectors. The thing to remember, however, is that to get the full glorious benefit of 5.1 digital surround sound from a DVD you will need a suitably equipped amplifier and the requisite number of speakers (five plus a bass unit called a sub-woofer).

Q **We often hear about the possible health risks of mobile phones, but what is the situation with phones such as the new cordless models we use at home?**

A There are a lot of concerned people around the world either researching or pressing for more research into the health issues surrounding all wireless devices. In the UK mobile phones are officially on a 'yellow card', with the publication of a report by Sir William Stewart, the government's chief scientific adviser, suggesting youngsters should at least be discouraged from using them regularly or for 'non-essential' calls. Research continues.

Meanwhile separate studies are pointing towards the fact that cordless phones actually emit around the same or even higher levels of ELF magnetic field pulses into the side of our heads and are always transmitting, unlike mobile phones which can be switched off. The bottom line again would seem to be use with caution. For an in depth discussion of the issues and technology surrounding the issue, check out *www.emfguru.org/* and Robert Bedard's excellent site *www.wave-guide.org/*.

Q I sometimes buy VHS videos from France, but they only play in black and white on my home set up. Is there any way round this?

A Our French neighbours use a video standard known as Secam, which although very similar to the UK's Pal system, has subtle differences in the way it processes colour information. Your best bet is either to upgrade your VCR to a multi standard one – look for a Pal/Secam label on the box – or have the movies converted professionally at somewhere like Alken MRS (*www.alkenmrs.com/video/standards.html*) which will cost around £16 per tape.

Q I've just purchased a complete home cinema system and would like to run three sets of speakers off the amplifier. How can I do this with only two output connectors?

A You can buy stereo speaker switch boxes (about £20 from retailers such as Maplin – *www.maplin.co.uk*) which allow you to run additional speakers to other parts of the house. Bear in mind, though, that you should check your amplifier specifications to see if your particular model will cope. Make sure also that you are happy with the quality of the switch, because the cheaper ones can reduce the overall sound quality.

Q What exactly are progressive scan TVs and should I think about getting one?

A The term relates to the way the television draws the picture on the screen. Most televisions interlace the image, that is they draw it in layers rather than all at once. A progressive scan or non-interlaced television screen operates much like a PC monitor, filling in the picture in one sweep giving a much crisper picture which is easier on the eye. In the future, all televisions will move to progressive scan to keep up with advances in high definition TV and DVD quality digital movies, but for now it remains more of an enthusiast's conversation piece. It's worth noting that flat-screen LCD and plasma televisions offer flicker-free progressive scan quality as standard – but at a price.

Q I recently bought a stereo system that includes a mini disk player. However, there seem to be very few recordings for sale in this format. Is there a future for this product?

A Sony certainly seems to think so, since it has spent the past decade or so pumping millions of dollars into marketing its invention to the world, albeit with patchy results. However, sales finally appear to be growing globally, especially in Japan, despite the relatively high price of the units and increasing competition from MP3 players and other formats. The bottom line is that mini disk almost certainly has a future as a superb portable digital recorder – witness the great professional mini disk recording products from Marantz – but perhaps not as a CD or DVD pre-recorded music replacement. Check out *www.minidisc.org* for more information.

Q I am looking to buy a rear projection TV but have been told the projection units or bulbs only last a small number of hours and are expensive to replace. Is this true?

A As far as I am aware the CRT projectors in most models last an equivalent amount of time to those in a conventional television, and the bulbs in LCD rear projection units are typically rated at between 4,000 and 8,000 hours. The amount of viewing time this gives will obviously depend on your own habits.

Q Why do so many recordable mini disks develop faults after being written over a couple of times?

A Mini disk recorders use a complex magnetic head and laser technology similar to CD-R, which is known to be sensitive to bad media and hardware misalignment problems. One possibility is that you are using cheap disks, which users have reported can be less reliable than more expensive ones. Try using the Sony brand for a while and see if the problem goes away. You could also have a duff record head or even laser unit. Get the shop where you bought the unit to test it thoroughly. There have been no reports of widespread unreliability in the mini disk format specifically as far as I am aware. You may find more information at *www.minidisc.org*.

Q On a couple of occasions recently I have set my VCR to record programs using the PDC facility, only to find out I have missed the first five or ten minutes. I don't feel that I can trust it anymore, what is going wrong?

A PDC (programme delivery control) is a system which allows video cassette recorders to start and stop at the precise time a programme is broadcast, rather than the times given in TV listings. It is especially useful for live programme overruns. Unfortunately, a lot of television services still do not fully support PDC because of reliability issues. Some older VCRs are also not fully PDC compliant, and a few early PDC transmissions are known to have been problematic.

Q I have a collection of old games on an Atari ST which we still enjoy playing. Is there a way of converting them to run on a standard PC?

A Ah yes, those wonderful days of primitive graphics and hiccupy sound but unmistakably enjoyable game play. Take a trip down memory lane by visiting *www.emulators.com/gemul8r.htm* where you will find what you need. Enjoy!

Q I have a large US DVD movie collection which I play on my Compaq laptop and which I have been told will not be able to play in the UK. I am relocating here shortly, so is this true?

A The quick answer is that your Compaq will continue to play them anywhere in the world. You will not, however, be able to play them on a UK-bought DVD player unless it is a multi-region model. Look around the shops to locate one or check out *www.codefreedvd.com* for more information.

10 · Best of the readers' tips

Cut your keystrokes

You can use the AutoCorrect command in Microsoft Word to reduce the number of keystrokes needed to enter text. To set up a short cut for your name and address, for instance, type the text, highlight it with the mouse, then select Tools – AutoCorrect. At the cursor type in the shortcut (eg na1), select Add then OK. Now when you type na1 followed by a space, the program will automatically convert it to your name and address in the text. Do not use real words as your shortcuts.

Reason for rebooting

If you are having trouble with your computer rebooting at random, it may be overheating. It is possible for the fan on the processor chip or power supply – especially on older systems – to stop working, making the temperature inside the case rise significantly. The added heat makes the CPU skip cycles, which can make the system reboot without warning.

Browse faster

You can speed up your web browsing simply by opening up more than one browser window and using them simultaneously. If you're using Microsoft's Internet Explorer it is much quicker to open a new window using the keyboard (press Control and N simultaneously) than to click on the browser icon.

Camera quality standard

Readers thinking of buying a digital camera should take into account the effect of image compression on the quality of the final printed image. A 1.3 megapixel camera designed to save the photos with very little file compression such as in TIF format will knock spots off all 2.1 megapixel and most 3.3 megapixel cameras which can only save their images in a highly compressed JPEG format. My 1.3 megapixel camera stores its shots in a fairly high compression JPEG format, while my friend's – also 1.3 megapixel – can save them with much less compression, giving a larger file size of 8MB but vastly better image quality.

PCs for students

New college students should always contact their computer or IT centre if they want to buy a PC. These centres often have special deals with local suppliers, reconditioned second-hand machines, or offer free or cheap extended maintenance. They may also know about special requirements or restrictions, such as a ban on certain products known to cause problems. Chest, the Combined Higher Education Software Team (*www.eduserv.org.uk/chest/*) also provides access to a huge range of discounted academic software.

Faster file opening

A quick and easy way to associate a file type with a particular program in Windows 98 is to highlight the name of the file in Windows Explorer and then right mouse click on it while holding down the shift key. You should then see a menu option saying 'Open with…' which will allow you to select the software you want to open the file. By ticking the box at the bottom of the next window – 'Always use this program…' you can also re-associate files that have been hijacked by other programs. This also works in Windows XP, but you don't need to hold down the shift key when clicking on the file name.

Easier website access

Windows 98 users who find a website they want to access often, can right click the mouse button when on the site and select 'Create shortcut'. This will place a shortcut to the site on their desktop, which they can either use from there or drag onto the Links section of their task bar for safe keeping and instant access. It's quicker and more convenient than searching through a list of bookmarks or favourites.

Redesign your desktop

To jazz up all your boring old Windows desktop themes, you can download free theme packs from *www.themeworld.com* ranging from television shows to celebrities and sports.

I have a Jimi Hendrix one. The site also contains fonts and screensavers which can be downloaded for free.

Boost your line capacity

Readers experiencing problems because of having too many devices connected to a home telephone line should consider installing a REN booster. These can be rented from BT or purchased from specialist electronics retailers for around £80. Another option is to consider a cordless telephone system which will allow up to five handsets on the one base station.

Beware minimum charges

When choosing an internet service provider, it pays to check the minimum call charges. British Telecom levies a minimum charge. If you mostly make brief calls to check email, this can make it much more expensive than some of the smaller companies.

Prevent disconnections

A good way to stop ISPs disconnecting you automatically if your browser is inactive for more than ten minutes when you are composing a lengthy email is to set the message checking option in Outlook Express to 'every two minutes'. Go to Tools – General – Check for New Messages. When viewing web pages, keep Outlook Express running but minimised, ensuring you won't be disconnected if you take a tea break.

Make the link quicker

Readers with a slow computer or internet connection may like to replace that annoying homepage which appears every time you open your browser. Simply create an HTML file in your word processing package which contains links to your favourite web addresses and store this on your hard drive. Locate and load the file in Internet Explorer by clicking File – Open – Browse and set it as your browser homepage (Tools – Internet Options – General – Home Page – Use Current) so every time you begin a browsing session you will start with a page full of links to your favourite sites.

Recycle promo CDs

I have finally found a use for all those free but unwanted promotional CDs that arrive almost daily in the post. I string them up over the soft fruit plants in my garden. The birds hate them and I have had my best crop of strawberries in ten years.

Incredible email

I would recommend an email program called Incredimail, which lets you have complete control over all aspects of your email. You can choose loads of letter styles, add animations and sounds and have a personal notifier that tells you when you've got mail while online. Check out the download at *http://incredimail.com.*

Don't kill the cookies

Having read about the use of cookies to spy on our surfing habits, I disabled them in my system. However, I subsequently found some sites refused to give me access, while others threw me off sharply or flashed up special messages. As a result, I have returned to my original cookies enabled setting. Readers should take note, therefore, that it may not be advisable to disable cookies completely.

Missing websites recovered

If you are ever trying to find a website which seems to have gone Awol, visit *www.google.com* and type the address or title into the search box. When the results come up, click on the link marked 'Cached' underneath the description. This is where Google very usefully stores its own copy of the websites it indexes, even if the original has temporarily gone missing.

Memory matters

Readers with slow machines should try upgrading the memory. I have found installing more memory (RAM) can produce a dramatic improvement in all-round performance.

Save time typing

For people keen to save time and keystrokes typing text,
I recommend a program called Shortkeys available at
www.shortkeys.com. It monitors your typing and every time
you enter a user-defined word or phrase it will replace it with
complete sentences or paragraphs. Useful for quickly
entering repetitive information such as addresses and other
regularly used blocks of text.

Better film transfers

Having transferred more movies from 8mm and 16mm to video
than I care to remember, I have realised that most movies are
projected at 24fps (frames per second) while video runs at
25fps. You should therefore ensure the transfer is made using
a 25fps projector, otherwise there will be bars on the video.

Browsing offline

Users of later versions of Internet Explorer under Windows
98 who want to save a web page to transmit, print or view
offline at their leisure, can select File – Save As and choose
the second Web Archive option. This will save the complete
page including text and graphic images to your hard disk in
a single file which can be accessed whenever you want.

Faster foreign connections

A good tip for those having problems connecting to the

internet with their modems while abroad is to go to Start –
Settings – Control Panel and select Modems – Properties –
Connection – Advanced – Extra Settings. Enter X3 in the box
provided and this will overcome any local line connection
problems. This can often help more than simply unchecking
the 'Wait for dial tone' box, which can cause problems of its
own.

Check your phone bill

A good way to track phone costs is to use BT's free Call My
Bill cost check service, which for some reason it doesn't
advertise. Dial 0800 854 608 and follow the instructions.
The service is updated daily at 10pm and will tell you how
much has accumulated on your bill since the last invoice.
You need to the customer code on your bill to access it, but
otherwise it's straightforward.

Easier Explorer updates

Want the latest version of Internet Explorer without the
lengthy download or taking up that 'free connection special
offer' which will leave weird icons and company branding all
over the place? Then browse one of those free CDs they send
out for Ie5setup.exe and click on the filename to run this and
update your system. You can check the version by a right
click over the file – look for a number like 5.50.4134.0600. If
the number is higher than the one you've got, you're in luck.

Break the read-only barrier

To convert a folder full of read-only documents, lasso them by dragging the cursor diagonally over the whole window till they all turn blue/selected. Then right click anywhere in the blue patch and select Properties. Then untick the read-only box and press OK. You will now be able to access the files as normal.

Free CD ROM warning

Beware of installing CD ROM giveaways. I recently tried to install a disk from a well-known fast-food chain and was left with a trashed Internet Explorer and Outlook Express and no way to uninstall. Don't use a disk unless it gives proper uninstall procedures and preferably a contact phone number in case of emergencies.

Get your email anywhere

Readers who want to access their email from around the world should try logging on to *www.twigger.co.uk*. All you have to do is supply your internet service provider user name and password.

Spread Word more effectively

Readers who have problems transferring Word documents to others should try saving them in another format before emailing them. For simple documents click File – Save As –

Text only. If you know the format of the recipient's word processor you can try saving the document to match that in the same way. This should also help readers who send documents created with older versions of Word to people running the latest version.

Make DVDs sound better

A great way to amplify the sound from your laptop when watching a DVD is to use one of those dummy cassette car adapters sold to convert CD Walkmans to in-car use. Plug the jack end of the cable into your laptop line out socket and the adapter end into any hi-fi, ghettoblaster or even – if you are out and about – car stereo cassette player that is at hand, and enjoy!

Online shopping warning

Beware when buying 'cheap' goods from overseas on the internet. I recently ordered some clothing from the US which looked considerably cheaper than similar items over here, even taking into account postage. However, the parcel arrived with a note attached from HM Customs & Excise charging import duty and VAT. Once the Royal Mail had added on its handling fee for collecting the amounts due I was out of pocket by an additional 35 per cent.

Waste less paper

I would recommend the Fineprint product which is available at *www.fineprint.com*. This printing program is excellent for web pages, creating small printed booklets and helps save trees by allowing you to print multiple pages of information on one sheet. I use it regularly and have found it easy and reliable. There is a free trial version available for download and the full version costs $29.95.

Glossary

Add-on/in A computer accessory that can be plugged into or attached to a PC by a cable or card, and which will upgrade the computer's functionality in some way. They include scanners, mice and sound cards. *See Peripheral*

Analogue The conventional means of moving and storing data using different electrical voltages. Examples include a television signal passing through an aerial.
See Digital

Application A software program designed for a particular purpose. For example a communications application can turn a PC into a sophisticated fax machine.

Back-up A copy of data or programs made by the user so that in the event of PC failure the information can be replaced allowing work to continue.

Benchmark A small utility program used to measure the performance and capabilities of computer hardware or software.

BIOS The basic input/output system of a computer. This is the set of programming code which translates the operating system into information the PC recognises.

Bitmap A graphics image format used extensively on PCs. Also known as BMP.

Boot The sequence of events, or start up process, when the PC is switched on. Most commonly involves loading an operating system.

Browser The software used to access the world wide web via the internet. The major brand is Microsoft's Internet Explorer.

Cache A form of buffer memory which enables information to be processed more quickly by the CPU or processor.

Card Add-in boards which can handle various tasks. Examples are graphics cards which drive the PC screen, sound cards which produce music and sound effects, and modem cards which let the PC 'talk' to a telephone or equivalent line.

CD ROM Compact disk read-only memory. A form of computer storage using 5-inch plastic disks and laser light reader drives. CDs are used for home audio as well as for computers. *See DVD*

Chip A small module, usually made of silicon, which incorporates an electrical circuit designed for a specific function. Examples include microprocessors, also known as CPUs (central processing units), such as the Pentium range from Intel Corporation.

Clip-art A selection of drawings used to add graphic impact to any word processed or other computer created document.

Clone A computer that mimics the operation of another. Examples include PC clones which mimic the original IBM Personal Computer. Note 'compatible' indicates the same thing. For example, IBM compatible software written to run on an IBM PC will work identically on the clone.

Consumables Items such as paper and inks used by computer peripherals such as printers.

Desktop computer A computer which fits onto the desktop, typically in an office environment.

DTP Desktop publishing. The process of laying out pages of text and graphics to create a publishable item. Typically done with a PC and software such as Adobe InDesign or QuarkXPress. Nowadays most word processing packages have a lot of the functions of traditional DTP packages and DTP specific software is mostly confined to high-end publishing requirements, such as magazine and newspaper production.

Digital The coding of information into a binary format which can be processed by a computer. Typically digital information can be compressed and manipulated much more easily than analogue so it is increasingly being used for applications such as broadcasting. Many traditional analogue formats, such as television and radio, are moving to a digital form. See *Analogue*

Disk crash The failure of a hard disk, which often results in loss of data stored on the computer.

Download To transfer information from one computer to another. Typical use is to download a file (eg a document) from one part of the internet onto the user's PC via the telephone line or equivalent.

DVD Digital versatile disks. The same size and appearance as CD ROMs, used for storing multimedia, software and data. They can hold around eight times more than a CD disk.

Email Electronic mail is a system for transferring messages from computer to computer using telephone lines or equivalent. Nowadays one of the major uses of the internet.

File A collection of recorded data. A program consists of files which interact to produce the application. Any user-generated information saved onto a disk (eg a letter) is saved in the form of a file. See *File format*

File format The different types of file used by software programs. For instance, a letter in Microsoft Word will be saved as a .doc file. This means the program can recognise it later when it needs to be re-opened. See *File*

Firewire Also known as IEEE 1394. A high speed data transfer and connection technology, similar to USB, which allows for transfer of information between devices using a specially designed cable. Now used extensively to transfer video and audio files between camcorders, music players, computers and other digital devices.

Floppy disk A form of computer storage in the form of a 3-inch disk in a plastic jacket. These can be used to supply software or to store back-up information. Becoming obsolete.

Graphics Diagrams, drawings or general artwork, including animation, produced on a computer either by the user or supplied as part of a game or other application software.

Graphics adapter Graphics or video card which handles the display of computer information on the screen.

Hard disk A permanently installed disk where user data and programs are stored. They have a very large capacity, so a number of programs and considerable amounts of data can be stored at the same time. Before hard disks became popular, programs were kept on floppy disks, which meant each one had to be individually loaded onto the PC every time it was required. See *RAM*

Icon A small image on a computer screen used to select an action such as starting a program.

Inkjet Form of printer where the ink is squirted onto the paper by small nozzles. Combines relatively high quality with low manufacturing costs. The standard method of reproducing photographic quality printouts at home. See *Laser printer*

Install To load a program or set of files onto a computer. The installation routine will put the program onto the hard disk for later access by the user.

Interface The point at which the computer hardware and external devices or users interact. For example, the printer port, where the printer cable is plugged into the computer, is the interface between the computer and the printer. Windows XP is the point at which the user and the computer interact. The Windows screen tells the user the actions they need to perform to accomplish a task, and the user will click on an icon on screen to do this. That is why Windows and other such screens are called GUIs, or graphical user interfaces.

Internet A sprawling and diverse collection of computers around the world connected via cable, satellite and radio transmissions. See *world wide web*

Joystick A games control device which resembles an aircraft joystick and operates by feeding signals into the computer in much the same way as a keyboard, but via a special joystick port.

JPEG Industry standard image format for photo files. It stands for Joint Photographic Experts Group (also abbreviated to JPG) and allows customisable compression so large photographic files can be transmitted, edited and stored more easily.

Laptop A portable computer small enough to be placed on the lap for working purposes. See *Notebook*

Laser printer Printer that uses laser light to generate text and images onto plain paper. Fast, quiet and now relatively inexpensive, they are the most popular form of printer for business use.

LCD Liquid crystal display used predominantly by small appliances such as watches, mobile phones and calculators. More sophisticated versions are found in laptop computers. Dual scan laptop LCD screens are relatively cheap to make but of lower quality than the more costly high resolution TFT or active matrix LCD colour screens.

Mail merge A word processing function, where one document can be addressed and sent to multiple recipients. A store of user inputted addresses are automatically inserted into the right place on each of the printed letters. Personalisation can include the salutation (Dear Bill, John, Mike, etc) as well as address and other information in the body of the letter.

Midi Musical instrument digital interface. This standard defines the way musical instruments such as synthesisers, and even non instruments such as tape recorders, can be connected to a PC to compose and arrange music. Most of the popular music industry uses the Midi interface in music studios.

MIPS Millions of instructions per second. A way of measuring and comparing computer performance.

Modem Modulator/demodulator. A device for converting the computer signal into information that can be transmitted down a telephone line. A modem at the other end will convert it back to computer talk so the destination computer can understand. Modems are used for both dial-up and broadband internet access.

MPEG The Motion Picture Experts Group format is one of the world's most popular digital video file formats. It uses advanced compression to make video files easier to transmit, edit and store.

Notebook computer Small laptop computer typically around the length and breadth of an A4 sheet of paper, hence the term notebook. See *Laptop*

Online Connected to another computer. This can be direct (computer to computer) but nowadays mostly refers to being connected to the internet. When we disconnect we are said to be offline.

Operating system The core software which makes the computer work in the first place. It tells the screen to light up, the keyboard to become active and all the other components to prepare for work. Examples include Microsoft's Windows XP or the Linux environment.

Peripheral A device which can be added to a basic computer system to perform a task. Examples are printers, scanners, plotters and external tape back-up units.
See *Add-on/in*

Pointing device A device for moving the action arrow or cursor around the screen of a PC. Examples are a mouse, trackball and touch pad.

Port A connection point or interface between the computer and an external device. Examples include the serial port used to connect things like external modems, and the parallel port commonly used to connect to a printer. Ports have standard fittings so peripherals from different manufacturers will all attach easily. See *Interface*

RAM Random access memory. The short-term storage area where programs run on a computer. The program (or a part of it) is loaded from the hard disk into this, where it starts running. As additional parts are needed they are loaded, a process which continues until the program is exited. See *Hard disk*

Scanner A device which takes an image on paper and converts it into code the computer can access and manipulate. Handheld scanners are commonly used for small images, while flat-bed versions are used for large amounts of information from books and other material.

Shareware Low-cost programs typically available from the internet or on CDs found free in magazines. They are offered on the basis that if you find them useful, you will pay the developer a fee which is usually around £40. There are thousands of these pieces of software and some companies have become very successful through this low-cost form of distribution. Freeware is the free version.

SIMM Single inline memory module. The format in which most modern RAM is sold. These are small boards which, when plugged internally into the PC, upgrade the amount of RAM. The right type of RAM must be used on the right type of SIMM, otherwise the upgrade may not work. See *RAM*

USB A standard data transfer technology which connects peripheral equipment such as keyboards, webcams, printers, modems and mice to computers. Nowadays it has almost completely supplanted all other forms of external attachment such as serial and parallel ports.

Utility Small software package that typically performs some routine task. Examples are anti-virus packages which check the computer regularly for infection by rogue software. See *Virus*

Virus Rogue software written to cause an undesired effect on the target computer. Infection can only take place through a direct connection to the target via cable, a floppy disk or other portable storage medium, or a network such as the internet.

Voice recognition Technology which lets users control their computers by talking to them and dictate information using a microphone and relevant software. Voice recognition (VR) software is improving but is still not sufficiently accurate or stable to be widely used as a replacement for the keyboard.

Voice over IP Technology which allows users to make and receive voice or video calls using a broadband internet connection. The advantages are low costs, with no per minute charging, especially on international calls and flexibility of service.

WiFi Wireless fidelity. A new technology designed to provide high speed data transfer for computers without using cables. Also known as wireless networking and 802.11.

Index